SPANISH DANCING
A Practical Handbook

SPANISH DANCING

A Practical Handbook

LALAGIA

Illustrations by Lyn Gray

Edited by Ana Ivanova

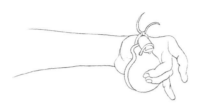

DANCE BOOKS

9 Cecil Court London WC2

First published 1985 by Dance Books Ltd.,
9 Cecil Court, London WC2N 4EZ
© *1985 by Lalagia*

y Princeton Book Co.,
·eton, N.J. 08540

Printers Ltd.,
·ridge, Hampshire

British Library Cataloguing in Publication Data

Lalagia
Spanish dancing: a practical handbook.
1. Dancing——Spain
I. Title   II. Ivanova, Ana
793.3′1946   GV1673

ISBN 0-903102-88-9

Dedicated with gratitude and admiration
to the memory of Antonia Merce 'La Argentina'
without whose help and that of my students
this handbook would not have been written

CONTENTS

CONTENTS

CONTENTS

CONTENTS

CONTENTS

INTRODUCTION

This handbook on Spanish dancing is an attempt simply to explain the basic exercises necessary for an elementary understanding and practice of the art. It is not an attempt to write history or to explain in any detail the many subtle differences of style or classification of dances, except in the broadest sense.

Such books as have been written on these subjects are recommended to anyone really interested. However, there is little detailed work in print which could be of practical help to beginners in the actual execution or understanding of the basic technique. Some students who may read this manual probably will have had training in classical ballet. This is essential for those who wish to learn classical Spanish dancing. For those who are chiefly interested in the regional and flamenco styles, a classical training is an advantage – although not a necessity.

The important point is the understanding of the correct use and direction of the weight of the body. Ballet training is geared to lift the weight upwards. Generally speaking, the opposite is the case in Spanish dancing (although there are some exceptions in *Baile de Zapatilla* and regional dances). This intrinsic fact should be understood from the first exercise as it is the basis upon which the movements are made. The essence of classical ballet movement is extrovert, light and outgoing, covering a wide space. On the other hand, Spanish dancing is chiefly introvert, inward looking, requiring comparatively little space.

The arm movements in ballet are open, in Spanish dancing they are closed and curved inwards round the body: in the former the whole impetus is outwards and upwards, inwards and downwards in the latter. The understanding of this relaxed and downward movement is fundamental to the correct execution of most steps in Spanish dancing, particularly in *Zapateado* and *Taconeo*.

13

INTRODUCTION

The method of instruction in this manual is my own which, after trial and error over many years of teaching, I have proved to be a useful groundwork, particularly for non-Spanish students from both Eastern and Western countries. The sequence of the exercises is in order of simplicity, beginning with the group on castanets, but it is not necessary to study all the castanet exercises before learning posture and position of the arms.

The best way, in my experience, is to practise the castanet exercises, then proceed to the posture and positions of arms and feet. When these are perfected, try to master *Braceo* 1 and *Taconeo* 1, and *Braceo* 2 and *Taconeo* 2, and so on until the *Taconeo Desplante* is reached. Only then is it time to try the *Zapateado* and following exercises. In this way, balanced progress will be achieved. However, before attempting any exercise, the notes under each heading should be thoroughly digested.

The main styles of Spanish dancing

Broadly speaking, Spanish dancing can be divided into three main styles or categories, each subject to its own subdivisions – Regional, Flamenco and Classical.

REGIONAL

Spain can be divided into five main regions: Northern, Southern, Central, Eastern and Western.

Briefly, the Basque dances and *Jotas* come from the North, the *Fandangos* from the South, the *Seguidillas* from the Centre and West, and the *Sardanas* from the East.

These dances are performed mostly by groups or couples and are danced by the ordinary people, amateurs, versed in their particular local dances which are a popular feature of the open air festivals. The dances from each region have their own particular and distinctive style which the professional dancer has to acquire and reproduce if the dance is to keep its special character, although the actual steps may be executed in a refined form.

The style varies tremendously according to the region. For example, the dances from the East are graceful, tranquil and of restrained expression; while those from the North are vigorous, almost rough in style, with a number of steps of elevation, the men vying with each other to see who can jump the highest. In direct contrast, the dances from the South are frequently individual, with the woman making sinuous and provocative movements, while the man shows his strength and virility, stamping upon the ground with his feet instead of leaping above it.

Spain is probably one of the richest countries in regional dances – Catalunia alone is said to have over three hundred. Often each small village has its own particular version. The study and correct execution of even some of these dances requires practice, time and effort.

FLAMENCO

Flamenco has long been a magic word for thousands of foreign tourists! Although the origin of these dances is obscure, they are supposed originally to have come from the ancient and sacred Hindu dances of India which, having lost their religious significance over the years, have become a more popular art form. During their travels westwards, eventually they entered Spain after having succumbed to Greek, Roman and Egyptian influences. According to Bonald: 'Flamenco dancing is Andalusian (i.e. regional) dancing which has been influenced by Asiatic and Arabic traditions which eventually combined and integrated with gipsy dancing'. It is an improvised art based on different types of music and dance which have developed in Southern Spain during the last few centuries. Flamenco flourished during the nineteenth century in *Cafe Cantante*, a type of café not unlike the French *Café Chantant* or the old English Music Hall, where one could drink and enjoy the entertainment.

The modern, sophisticated and more respectable equivalent is the *Tablao* or traditional flamenco show where drinks are served and the artists appear on a small stage, usually sitting in a half circle whilst they perform songs and dances amid shouting, clapping and the snapping of fingers, accompanied by the playing of guitars and castanets. The latter are a comparatively new feature among the gipsies. Improvisation is rare. This is a theatrical presentation. Today one may be lucky to find a high-quality performance in the theatre, exemplified by Mario Maya's *Ay Jondo* or Antonio Gades *Carmen*, but even in the caves of Granada the usual routine for tourists is of low standard. Sometimes it is possible to be present at a special cave show or *juerga* (party/binge), where gipsy art at a high peak of improvisation and expression may still be enjoyed.

Gipsy songs to which the dances are allied have two aspects – the *Cante Jondo* (profound song) and *Cante Chico* (little song). The first, as the name suggests, is serious, extolling human emotions, the cry of the oppressed which in the case of the dance projects itself into movement. The second is gay, light and often humorous and for this reason making an immediate appeal. It is, therefore, popular with the average audience.

The principal dances of the *Cante Jondo* are: *Alegrias*, *Soleares*, *Seguiriya*, *Zapateado*, and *Caña*.

The dances of the *Cante Chico* are: *Farruca*, *Bulerias*, *Tangos*, *Zambras*, *Zorongo*, *Caracoles*, *Garrotin*, and *Rumbitas*.

CLÁSICO ESPAÑOL

The classical dances are a synthesis of regional and *Flamenco* styles plus a form of eighteenth-century ballet technique evolved by the Italians. According to the Italian dancing master Magri, the Spaniards learnt to dance in the Italian manner, adding to it their own jumped and beaten steps to the sound of castanets. This was the great Spanish contribution to eighteenth-century classical technique. Artistically, these dances are the most complete, requiring a long academic training, a highly developed understanding of music and great skill in playing the castanets.

During the seventeenth century, dances based on folk, religious and aristocratic dances began to find expression in a type of theatre called a *Corral* (an open air playhouse surrounded by houses). Dancing masters held an esteemed position in society at this time; indeed, the above-mentioned Magri was the Spanish king's dance master for classical ballet technique. During the period of French and Italian influences, the *Baile de Zapatilla* or slipper dances were born of Spanish parentage.*

The dances were based on a form of classical ballet technique called *Escuela Bolero*. They first appeared in the middle of the eighteenth century and became extremely popular, possessing not only the refinement and elegance of the Court, but also the best academic dancing of this period. The *bolero* in particular was danced in numerous forms: for couples, for groups or as a solo. It usually consisted of three verses: an introduction, adornment and exaltation. Some steps are danced together, others singly to show off the technical virtuosity of each individual artist to good advantage while retaining the graceful use of the arms. Until quite recently, some theatres

---

*See *Dancing Spaniards* by Ana Ivanova.

and cabarets engaged a *Cuadro Bolero* as well as a *Cuadro Flamenco*, each making its own specialised presentations. Since flamenco has become so popular among foreigners, the *Cuadro Bolero* has almost died out, although lately there seems to be a revival of interest.

During the nineteenth century, dances of the *Escuela Bolero* became extremely popular in Europe, performed by well-known ballerinas, many of whom went to Spain especially to learn them. This was during a time of actual decline in the quality of dancing in the peninsula itself. Just before this decline came the dances from the *Zarzuela*, a light-hearted type of operetta. This typically Spanish art form flourishes today and Madrid has a theatre named after it.

Under the heading *Clásico Español* are the regional dances as well as the neo-classical style of the concert artist. This style was promoted by the famous dancer Antonia Mercé '*La Argentina*', who was the first to use Iberian classical composers in her recitals. She interpreted their music with unerring taste and unsurpassed playiang of the castanets.

A classical dancer is expected to excel in at least one of the above-mentioned styles and to the conversant with all. The principal dances of the *Escuela Bolero* are *boleros* in great variety, such as:

Bolero Seco
Bolero liso
Bolero de medio paso
Bolera con cachucha
Bolero robado
Bolero popular

Seguidillas

Fandangos
   Olé
   Jaleo

CASTANETS

Castanets are a musical instrument of great antiquity, dating back to the time of the ancient Egyptians for certain, and even earlier in the form of primitive clappers. Probably they were introduced into Spain during the first century AD.

For those interested in the history of castanets there is an excellent book called *Woods that Dance* by Matteo (see Bibliography). Until this was published, in English little contemporary material had been written on the art and origin of castanet playing.

Castanets for professional dancers are carved out of various woods; granadillo, ebony and a man-made material called *tela* are considered to be the best. The carver is called a *palillero*.

Castanets are made in several sizes to suit the dancer's hand and are fastened together with a cord, the thickness of which is important to the correct sounding of the instrument. Castanets for men are larger and more sonorous than those made for women. They are male (*macho*) and female (*hembra*), have a high and low tone and are tuned so that the left hand is a musical third lower than the right. The male or low tone is played on the left hand which strongly marks the rhythm, while the *caretillas* and the counter rhythms played on the right hand adorn the sound.

Mass-produced castanets for the tourists have a poor tone and are usually strung with a thin red and yellow cord decorated with pompoms. If these are the only ones available, they can be used by beginners for practice providing the string is removed and a thicker one is substituted. It should be about twelve inches in length and thick enough just to thread through the holes.

THREADING THE CASTANETS TOGETHER
Starting with the left, having first tested the castanet for deep tone, insert the end of the cord through both holes on the left side of the

18

instrument, then pass the cord through the other two holes of the right side of the same castanet. Now both ends of the cord are on the same side. Make a slip knot with one end, through which you insert the other cord, but do not tighten it too firmly at present. Knot the two ends of cord separately to prevent fraying. Adjust the right-hand castanet similarly in reverse. You are now ready to put on the castanets. Should the cords loosen during practice you can tie the two ends in a second knot close to the first knot.

PUTTING ON THE CASTANETS

Put the knotted side of the loop over the slightly flexed left-hand thumb joint and slip the first loop over the thumbnail. The knot must be nearest the hand and on top. Now tighten the slip knot and adjust the cord by pulling it so that the castanet hangs securely from the thumb and rests on the palm of the hand. You will notice that the thumb is bent; as you attempt to straighten it the castanet will move away from the hand.

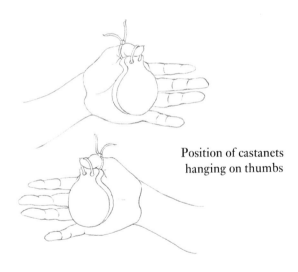

Position of castanets
hanging on thumbs

Fig. 1. How to put on the castanets

When trying the first beat (*golpe*), it will be observed that there is an important relationship between the position of the thumb and the fingers making the beat. The slight flexing of the joint adjusts the position of the castanet so that the tension between the two is exactly right for ease of playing, clarity and strength of sound. You will be able to judge this for yourself as you progress.

CASTANET SOUNDS

The different sounds that are made on the castanets are named as follows (R = right; L = left):

Ta	Single beat with L
Ti or pi	Single beat with R
Pita	Single beat with R then L
Riá	Roll with R finishing with single beat L
Postiseo	Knocking castanets together
Cop	Single beat on both hands played together
Golpe	beat
Caretilla	roll

HOW TO MAKE A GOLPE

Starting with the L hand, palm facing inwards with the castanet hanging on the L thumb joint, strike the castanet sharply with the cushioned tips of the two middle fingers. Strike the middle of the castanet with slow, even beats, but do not straighten the fingers from their curved position nor move the wrist. Practise 6 slow beats followed by 6 quicker ones.

In the same way repeat the above with the R hand. Practise many times, remembering to flex the thumb joint to the most convenient

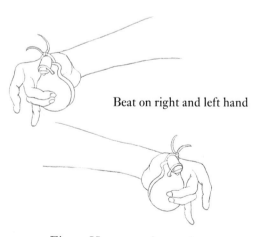

Beat on right and left hand

Fig. 2. How to make a *golpe*

position in which to make the beat. After practising the above, make a *golpe* with the L hand and a *golpe* with the R.

Count:

1	2	3	4
L	R	L	R

Now try the following:

Golpe L, *Golpe* R, *Golpe* L

Count:

1	2	3	4
L	R	L	hold*

Repeat several times, then repeat starting from the R.

Most of the following castanet exercises can be practised sitting down. In fact, it aids concentration to do so in the early stages. However, as soon as you can play a simple rhythm it is wise to practise standing in the positions indicated at the beginning of the exercises. This will gradually accustom you to think of this posture as well as your castanets.

Before practising any of the exercises in a standing position, see notes on posture and positions of the arms (p. 30). The castanets can be practised in the order in which they are written. It will not be possible to do the more difficult exercises until the early ones have been mastered. You will notice, however, that the use of the castanets with arm movements is only very gradually introduced in the simplest possible way, such as a single beat on the left hand, or a *cop* on a given count. Proceed slowly. Take the first practise as a guide for the future; having perfected it to the best of your ability start on the next three exercises of *Braceo* and *Taconeo*, and so on, until you reach those exercises using both feet and arms together.

SIMPLE CASTANET EXERCISE FOR MAKING A GOLPE

With arm and wrist still, execute single beats with the two middle fingers of the L hand, slowly at first, then as quickly as possible, but always keeping an even rhythm.

---

*On the 4th beat both castanets are held firmly against the palm, only to be released in order to make the next beat. This is important as it keeps control of the instrument and prevents clicks at the wrong moment, so remember to hold the castanets unless you are actually making a beat.

CASTANETS

Position of castanets

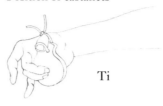

Ti

Fig. 3. Simple castanet exercise for making a *golpe*

Count:

I	a	2	a	3	a	4	a	*ad lib.*
ta,	ta,	ta,	ta,	ta,	ta,	ta	ta	

Repeat with R

I	a	2	a	3	a	4	a	*ad lib.*
ti,	ti,	ti,	ti,	ti,	ti,	ti,	ti	

Now repeat with the L hand, making the beats as loud and as strong as you can, gradually diminishing the sound until the beats are quiet, though retaining clarity and rhythm.

Repeat with R.

WRIST EXERCISE FOR COP
With the palm of the L hand facing inwards and wrist unbroken, hold the castanets against the palm with the two middle fingers. Bend the wrist inwards slightly towards the body, then sharply bend it

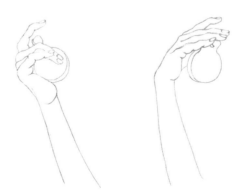

Figs. 4 & 5. Wrist exercise for *cop*

outwards back to its original position, taking care that you stop the outward movement before the wrist line is broken.

Practise several times with both hands.

Count:

and 1   and 2   and 3   and 4
in, out, in, out, in,   out, in,   out

When you find this wrist movement easy, try making a beat as follows: Starting with the L hand in the same position as for *golpe* and with the middle fingers curved poised to strike, bend the wrist slightly inwards, then bend the wrist outwards and at the same time strike the castanet with the middle fingers. It is as if you were trying to throw the castanets out of your hand but the fingers making the beat prevent you from doing so. Remember the beat is made on the outward movement. The wrist returns to its unbroken position.

Practise slowly with each hand, counting as before:

and   1   and   2   and   3   and   4
flex   strike flex   strike flex   strike flex   strike

Practise 16 times with each hand separately.

HOW TO MAKE A COP
The *cop* is made by striking the castanets with both hands at the same time in the same way as in the previous exercise.

Slightly flex wrist inwards (to give impetus) then make a single

Fig. 6. Position for *cop*

23

beat outwards on both hands together, finishing without a broken wrist line.

You should now be holding both castanets pressed against the palms of the hands by the middle fingers.

Flex wrists at the same time, relax fingers and let go of castanets. You are now ready to make another beat.

Remember, this slight wrist movement is used on the *cop* to emphasise the beat and should not be used on ta or ti as a general rule. Also remember the strike is always on the outward movement.

With arms extended as in Fig. 6 and palms facing, practise slowly with both hands together, counting as before.

Count:

and	1	and	2	and	3	and	4
flex	strike	flex	strike	flex	strike	flex	strike

Practise 16 times.

The Caretilla

The *caretilla* or roll is one of the most important features in castanet playing. Technically, it is a continuous roll of five beats produced by the four fingers of the right hand striking the treble castanet successively, followed by a single beat on the left hand.

As the little finger strikes the castanet first, it is called the first or 1. The ring finger is second or 2. The middle finger is third or 3. The index finger is fourth or 4, being the fourth to hit the castanet. The *caretilla* is made by using the short nail tips of the 1st, 2nd and 3rd fingers, while the 4th or index finger holds the castanet against the palm after making the beat.

Practise, starting with the little finger using the tip, hit the castanet sharply with a plucking movement, sliding the finger inwards as it curls under the hand. This is followed immediately by the second and third fingers in the same manner, followed by the fourth which hits the castanet with the flat, rather than the tip, of the finger (see Fig. 7).

To begin with, you may find this movement of the fingers quite difficult. Remember to adjust the thumb by flexing the joint to the easiest position so that the tension between the thumb and finger making the beat is exactly right. Aim to make slow, clear beats.

CASTANETS

Count:

1	2	3	4
1st	2nd	3rd	4th

Continue to repeat this sequence on the R hand until you gain confidence. The following exercise will help strengthen the fingers.

CASTANET EXERCISE FOR THE CARETILLA

Starting with the first or little finger and using the tip, hit castanet sharply with a plucking movement, sliding the little finger inwards. Repeat the same movement with the second or ring finger – using only these fingers repeat many times.

Count:

a	1	a	2	a	3	a	4
1st	2nd	1st	2nd	1st	2nd	1st	2nd
beat,	*beat*,	beat,	*beat*,	beat,	*beat*,	beat,	*beat*

Note the accented beats.

Repeat this exercise using the second and third fingers only.

Repeat this exercise using the third and fourth fingers only.

During the above exercise hit the castanet as hard as you can in order to strengthen the fingers.

HOW TO MAKE A CARETILLA

Make a beat with the two middle fingers of the L hand and in the

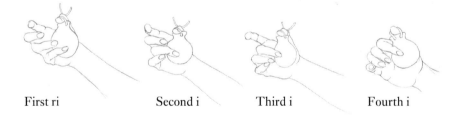

First ri   Second i   Third i   Fourth i

ta and á   beginning and end of *caretilla*

Fig. 7. How to make a *caretilla*

same way as before make beats with the first, second, third and fourth fingers of the R hand, followed by a single beat on the L.

Count:

I	2	a	3	a	I	2	a	3	a	I
ta	ri -	i -	i -	i -	á	ri -	i -	i -	i -	á
L (R)	1st	2nd	3rd	4th	L (R)	1st	2nd	3rd	4th	L

Practise slowly, making each beat clear and distinct. The second or ring finger is usually the weakest and needs extra practice. The transition from the beat on the L hand to the roll on the R and back to the L must be made without any pause or difference in sound, excepting the count of I which is accented in the above exercise. The beats should sound even.

Do not be too ambitious at this stage by trying to make a fluid roll. Continue to practise making each beat stacatto and separate; this is called *golpeando*.

Practise daily until the fingers become flexible – when this has been achieved the time has come to try making a fluid and continuous roll called *rasgueando*. This will only come after a great deal of practice, so if you find it difficult, return to making each beat separately as before. Then try this simple exercise:

Count:

I	a	2	a	3	I	a	2	a	3
ta		riá		riá	ta		riá		riá

Note in this exercise the roll begins on 'a' and ends with the beat on the L hand on the counts 1, 2, 3.

Postiseo

The easiest way to make the correct position for practising *postiseo* is to place the hands in front of you with palms facing, fingertips together facing forwards.

Turn R wrist until tips of R fingers face upwards, fingers gracefully curved, which should be retained throughout the exercise. In this position knock the castanets together: you have then made *postiseo*. Separate the hands enough to make one *golpe* R and one *golpe* L = *Postiseo*, ti, ta.

CASTANETS

Fig. 8. Exercise for *postiseo*

Count:

and	*postiseo*
a	ti
1	ta
and	*postiseo*
a	ti
2	ta

EXERCISE FOR POSTISEO WITH A SIMPLE ARM MOVEMENT

note: See notes on posture and positions of the arms (p. 30) before doing this exercise.

Face　= front
Feet　= in 4th
Arms　= relaxed at side, with elbows held up, shoulders relaxed, chest expanded

To make postiseo, cop:
Count:

a 1	Gracefully bring arms forward to 5th down in front and make *postiseo, cop* (*postiseo* on a, *cop* on 1)
a 2 a 3	Bring arms back to 5th down back, ready to make *postiseo cop* behind the back on count:
a 1	(*postiseo* on a, *cop* on 1) Repeat *ad lib.*

As the arms open to the side and close on the *postiseo* they should swing naturally, curved but relaxed. Avoid tensions when making the *postiseo*.

Castanet rhythms

SIMPLE RHYTHMS – JOTA ARAGONESA
Position for practice – see Fig. 6. Feet together. Arms curved slightly upwards in 2nd.

Count:

1 bar	1	2	a	3	
	Cop	ta	ti	ta	
	together	L	R	L	Repeat *ad lib.*

2 bars	1	2	a	3,	1	a	2	3	
	Cop	ta	ti	ta,	ta	ti	ta	cop	Repeat *ad lib.*

BASIC RHYTHM – SEVILLANA

1 bar	1	a	2	á	3	a,	
	ta	ri	á	ri	á	pi,	Repeat *ad lib.*

BASIC RHYTHM – FANDANGO

$3\frac{1}{4}$ bars

1	&	a	2	&	a	3	&	a	1
ta,	ta	ri	á,	ta	ri	á	riá	ri	á
&	a	2	&	a	3	&	a	1	
ta	ri	á,	ta	ri	á	riá	ri	á	
&	a	2	&	a	3	&	a	1	
ta	ri	á,	ta	ri	á	riá	ri	á	etc.

Note: After the first bar the count of 'a 1' is riá. The position of the arms in 2nd, curved slightly upwards, is a feature of some regional dances and for beginners is an easy position in which to practise.

MUSIC – PASADOBLE

Count:

1 bar	1	&	a	2	&	a	3	&	a	4	&	a	
	*t*a,	ta	ti	*t*a,	ta	ti	*t*a,	ta	ti	*t*a,			Repeat *ad lib.*

Note: Counts are strongly accented.

1 bar	1	&	a	2	&	a	3	&	a	4	&	a	
	*t*a,	ta	ri	*á*,	*t*a	ri	*á*,	*t*a	ri	*á*			Repeat *ad lib.*

MUSIC – MALAGUEÑA
Simple exercise to be used with *Braceo* (arm exercise).

CASTANETS

Count:

2 bars	1	a	2	a	3	a,	4	a	5	a	6	a
	ta	ti,	ta	ti,	ta	ti,	ta	ti,	ta	ti,	ta	ti,

	1	a	2	a	3	a	4	a	5	a	6	a
	ta	r i	á	r i	á	pi,	ta	r i	á	r i	á	pi

Count six for each circle of arms.

MUSIC – PRELUDE (Albeniz)

Count:

1 bar	1	a	2	a	3	a	4	a	5	a	6	a
	ta	ta,	ti	ti,	ta	ta,	ti	ti,	ta	ta,	ti	ti

Count twelve for each circle when this music is used for *Braceo* I.

POSTURE AND POSITIONS OF THE FEET AND ARMS

Positions of the Feet (See Fig. opposite – Positions of the feet)

In modern Spanish dancing the five positions of the feet are similar to those in classical ballet,* but only slightly turned out and with knees relaxed in a natural position.

　1st　position = heels together
　2nd　position = the length of the foot apart (weight even)
　3rd　position = heel against arch of other foot
　4th　position = one foot in front of the other
　5th　position = front heel to back toe

Standing erect, the weight of the body is evenly distributed between the two feet and from the hips downwards the limbs are relaxed. Above the waist there should be a feeling of stretching the body upwards while expanding the chest and holding the back straight with arms and shoulders completely relaxed, but with upheld elbows. In both posture and movement, the importance of the carriage of the body cannot be underestimated: each part of the body must be balanced and in correct line with the rest.

　N.B. Some Spanish and some French terms are used where it is thought they will be helpful to the student.

---

*For the *Escuela Bolero* the five positions of the feet are those used in classical ballet.

POSITIONS OF THE FEET

Feet together   First position   Second position   Third position

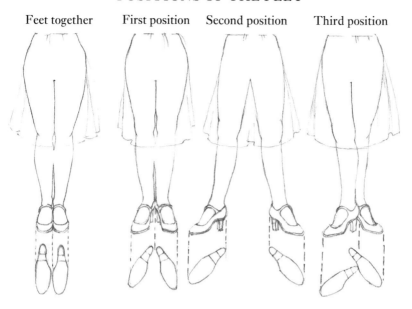

Fourth position   Fifth position   *Planta natural*

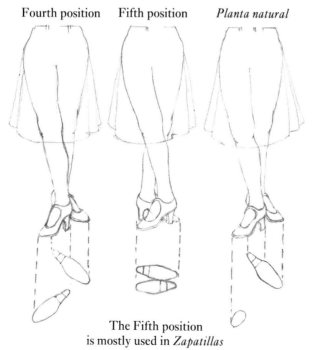

The Fifth position
is mostly used in *Zapatillas*

Positions of the feet

Positions of the arms (See Fig. opposite – Positions of the arms)

1st =	Arms curved in front of chest, carried lower than the shoulders, palms facing, rounded elbows held higher than the waist.
2nd =	Arms open to side, slightly below shoulder level and slightly curved with palms facing front, elbows held up.
3rd =	R arm curved above head framing face, L arm rounded to side in 2nd, or vice versa.
4th =	R arm curved above head, L arm curved across chest facing centre point of body, or vice versa.
4th *Baja* (down) =	R arm in 1st, L arm curved behind back.
5th =	Both arms curved above head framing the face, palms facing.
5th *Delante* (in front) =	Both arms down, curved in front over thighs, palms facing.
5th *Detras* (behind) =	Both arms down, curved behind back, palms facing.

Arm movements flow into each other through the various positions, which must co-ordinate with the rest of the body movement at all times.

N.B. When describing the movement of a working arm, the positions through which it passes will not be in relation to the arm which is still.

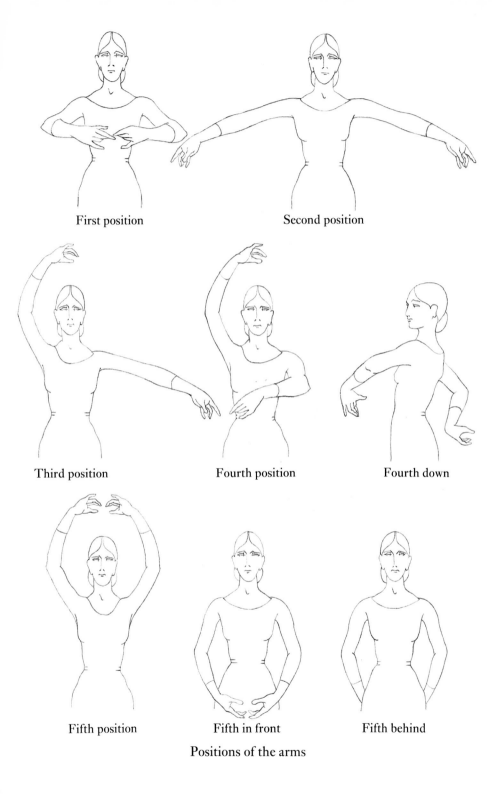

First position

Second position

Third position

Fourth position

Fourth down

Fifth position

Fifth in front

Fifth behind

Positions of the arms

BRACEO (Carriage of the arms)

The arms frame the head and/or body of the dancer, passing through a series of varying positions, each of which must be seen in correct co-ordination with the feet, and with each other, so that there is a continuous flow of movement. It should be remembered that the arm moves from the shoulder to the fingertips, and that the whole movement should be fluid, flowing from one position to another, always maintaining a curved line.

Grace of movement and simplicity, with purity of line, should be the aim. This is by no means easy to acquire, but it is helpful to remember that usually the shoulders and hips are in line, the back straight with head held high and looking naturally at the audience or to either side as the step requires. Sometimes the arms are still while expression of feeling is portrayed by rotating the wrists and flexing the fingers.

The natural pride and developed ego of the Spaniard requires the dancers to have a definite and positive approach to their work. A confident bearing is essential, but this does not mean an overemphasis of posture. This is a mistake often made by beginners and sometimes by ballet dancers with a false idea of Spanish line. For example, the effective posture to end a phrase is obtained by the sudden cessation of movement at a given moment rather than by the striking of an attitude. Sudden changes of rhythm and mood need to be felt, not simulated.

It is wise first to study and perfect the simple exercises so that a basis is made on which to build.

Avoid all exaggerations and affectations. All positions must be clearly shown. Jerky movements and angular elbows are ugly.

Do not try to take the arms too far behind the head in early exercises, as undue strain may cause the shoulders to rise and the head to poke forward.

The basic arm exercises should be learnt before attempting to use them with the castanets and they should be practised until they become second nature. You can then concentrate on the castanets.

It is expedient to begin by only playing the L castanet as it usually marks the rhythm, then as progress is made gradually introduce the R hand.

At first it may be found that there is a tendency to jerk the arms when playing and that there is difficulty in spacing the movements to fit the counts. Therefore, these faults must be avoided at all costs to ensure a smooth and flowing movement.

Advice to the pupil on the first practice

Before starting your first real practice, study the notes on posture, learn the positions of the feet and arms and try to perfect them in front of a mirror so that you can compare the positions with the illustrations to see that they are correct. Then sit down and practise the first exercises for *Golpe*, *Cop* and *Caretilla*, as directed.

Before attempting *Braceo* I, face the mirror and be sure that you are standing correctly. At first, practise *Braceo* I without body or head movement, concentrating on the arms. When you have avoided the obvious mistakes, try using the slight inclinations of the body with arm movements, watching yourself so that you keep the correct line. Finally, introduce the head movement. The exercise may seem difficult for your first practice, but it is the skeleton, so to say, upon which all the arm movements are based and is, therefore, very important.

It is wise to build on a solid technical foundation, so try to practise and understand each exercise before attempting the next one.

As you progress, introduce the more difficult exercises, but only very gradually, particularly the *Zapateado*, which is best left until the *Taconeo* is thoroughly understood. The castanests can be practised in the order in which they are written. It will not be possible to do the more difficult exercises until the early ones have been mastered. However, you will notice that the use of the castanets combined with the arm movements is only very gradually introduced, as for example a single beat on the L hand or *cop* on a given count.

Progress slowly, take the first practice as a guide for the future. Having perfected it to the best of your ability, start on the next three exercises of *Braceo* and *Taconeo*, and so on, until you reach those exercises using both the feet and arms together.

Preparation for Braceo I

Standing erect, face front, feet in 4th position, weight mostly on back foot. Arms relaxed, hanging loosely at side with shoulders relaxed, and chest expanded. Curve the elbows away from body while bringing arms upwards and outwards through 2nd position to 5th.

Figs. 1 & 2. Preparation for *Braceo* I

Braceo I

Count:

> Down 1 2 3   Up 4 5 6

Gently stroking the air with the fingertips, circling outwardly with the R arm passing through the 2nd position downwards to 5th in front, then bringing same arm slightly across chest, upwards through the 1st position, returning to 5th; always keeping the arms slightly curved and relaxed, elbow on top, palms facing. Repeat with L arm.

Now repeat the whole exercise, circling inwards through the 1st position to 5th down in front, continuing outwards through 2nd upwards to 5th.

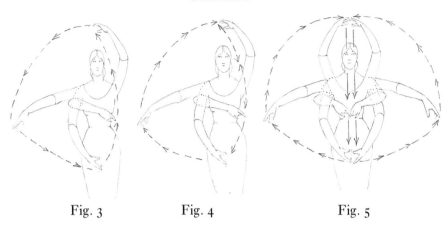

Fig. 3   Fig. 4   Fig. 5

Now both arms make an inward circle, coming forwards and down-wards to 5th in front, then outwards and upwards through 2nd to 5th, then continue the movement by making outward circle through 2nd to 5th in front and upwards through 1st to 5th.

Now practise *Braceo* I using the head and body as follows:

OUTWARD MOVEMENT
On the count of 1, the head and eyes move naturally to the R, at the same time the body is slightly inclined to the L away from the working arm; look to the front as the body is brought erect on the count of 4.

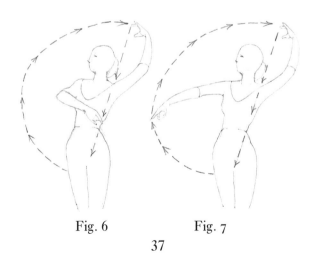

Fig. 6   Fig. 7

INWARD MOVEMENT

Counting and head movements are as above; the arm coming slightly across the chest makes a relaxed and fluid movement at all times. When both arms make the inward circle, the body inclines to R, eyes to L, then back to position facing front as the arms travel outwards and upwards to 5th.

Vice versa on outward movement.

Counting 6 beats for each circle as before.

PITFALLS TO AVOID

Failing to observe the exact positions of the body and arm movements as the exercise demands, e.g., bent elbows.

Holding arms too far forward or forcing them too far back instead of naturally framing the face.

Raising the shoulders.

Failing to pass through the positions indicated by curtailing the movement, dropping the elbow and passing the arm too close to the body.

Overextending the arms so that they are not rounded.

Contracting the fingers and arm muscles.

Lack of fluidity in movement.

It is wise to develop grace and softness in the movement of the fingers, which should be grouped together naturally with the middle fingers slightly rounded (see hand positions).

Planta Natural (exercise to change weight)

See also Fig. – Positions of the feet.

Face front.

Feet together.

Arms relaxed at side.

Extend R foot to 4th front and let it rest on ball of slightly turned out foot.

Bring R foot back, feet together, change weight on to R and extend L in similar manner.

The weight must be changed as smoothly as possible, allowing the hips to move naturally on the transition.

Avoid a bobbing movement up and down.

BRACEO

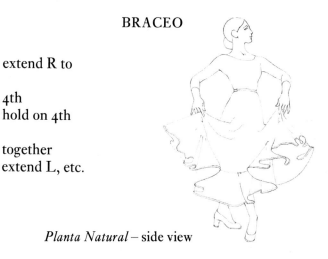

Count:
- **&** extend R to
- **a**
- **1** 4th
- **&** hold on 4th
- **a**
- **2** together
- **&** extend L, etc.
- **a**

Planta Natural – side view

Braceo for simple held positions

A   *Arms* (from 1st to 4th). Feet *Planta Natural* R front

Count:
- **a** Raise arms forward into 1st and make *postiseo*, looking at hands

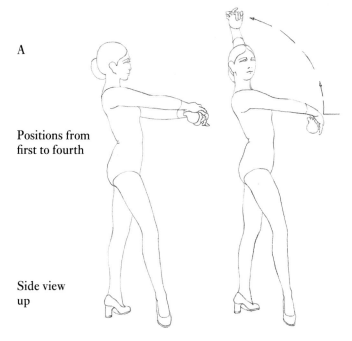

A

Positions from
first to fourth

Side view
up

Figs. 1 & 2. *Braceo* for simple held positions

1   move R arm up to 4th position making *cop*, and look at L corner
2   hold
3   make *postiseo* in 1st, looking at hands,
1   move L arm up into 4th, making *cop*, look at R corner
2   hold
3   repeat as above *ad lib.*, taking care to hold the correct positions

B   *Arms* (from 1st to 4th down)

Count:
a   Raise arms forward into 1st and make *postiseo*, looking at hands
1   turn and look diagonal R, arms in 4th down R front, making *cop*
2   hold
3   face front, make *postiseo* in 1st, looking at hands
1   turn and look diagonal L, arms in 4th down L front, making *cop*
2   hold
3   repeat as above

B

Positions from
first to fourth down

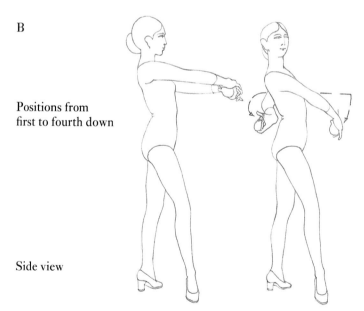

Side view

Figs. 3 & 4. *Braceo* for simple held positions

BRACEO

Note : Remember the R over L hand position in *postiseo*.

C   *Arms* (from 5th to 4th down)
Face and look front.

Count:

a   Raise arms upwards through 2nd to 5th and make *postiseo*

1   turn and look diagonal R, arms in 4th down, R front and make *cop*

2   hold

3   raise arms upwards through 2nd to 5th and make *postiseo*, at the same time turn to look and face front.
Repeat as above to L

Feet

Position of body = face front
Feet = in 1st position

C

Count:

a   Change weight onto R

1   point L 4th front (*planta natural*)

2   hold

3   bring L into 1st

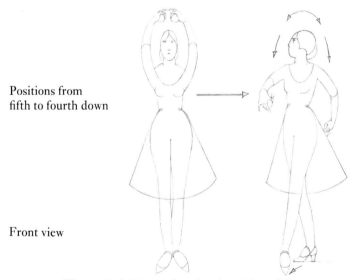

Positions from
fifth to fourth down

Front view

Figs. 5 & 6. *Braceo* for simple held positions

41

1 point R 4th front
2 hold
3 repeat as above, changing the feet smoothly with relaxed knees

Repeat as above, slightly turning the body to diagonal R and L in 4th position, keeping hips and shoulders in line. Facing front on change of weight.

Braceo II

Position of body = diagonal (R shoulder to R corner)
Feet = 4th position R to front
Look = to R corner
Arms = 5th behind, palms facing each other
Castanets: *Postiseo Cop*. Count a 1 a 2 a 3.

Raise arms upwards and outwards, through 2nd to 5th, at the same time bend slightly from above the waist to R corner whilst turning head to look at L corner (diagonal).
Castanets: *Postiseo Cop*. Count a 4 a 5 a 6.

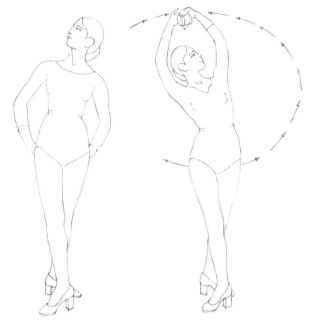

Figs. 1 & 2. *Braceo* II

Lower arms downwards through 2nd to 5th behind, at the same time bend towards L (diagonal) looking to R.

Repeat slowly several times.

CASTANETS

Count:

a	1	a	2	a	3
Postiseo cop		ta	riá	ta	riá
a	4	a	5	a	6

PITFALLS TO AVOID

Failing to keep the diagonal line of arms, head, shoulders and hips.

Allowing the head and shoulders to poke forward when the arms are in 5th behind.

Bending forwards instead of sideways.

Dropping and bending elbows.

Braceo III

Figs. 1, 2 & 3. *Braceo* III

43

BRACEO

Position of body, etc. – as for *Braceo II*.

Count:

a 1		*Postiseo Cop*
a 2 a 3		raise arms upwards and outwards to 2nd and forwards to 1st
a		*Postiseo*
4		*Cop*, raising R arm to 4th
a 5 a 6		holding arms in 4th position

Repeat exercise to L

Note: On count of

a 1 a 2 a 3	look to R corner (front)
a	look at hands
4 a 5 a 6	look to L corner (front)

CASTANETS

Count:

a	1	a	2	a	3
Postiseo cop		ta	riá	ta	riá
a	4	a	5	a	6

PITFALLS TO AVOID

Dropping the elbows in the 1st position, thus losing the downward sloping line from the shoulders.

Failing to extend the arm in the 4th (i.e., bent elbows) when upper arm should frame the head.

Dropping the chin in 4th when you should look up.

Braceo IV (A)

Position of body = face front
Feet = 4th front, weight on L, R *planta natural*
Look = to L corner (front)
Arms = in 5th, inclining body to R
In this position make the following hand and castanet exercise, with R hand over L for the *postiseo*.

Count:

	&	a	1	&	a	2	&	a	3	&	a	4
Castanets:	Pos*	ti	ta,	pos	ti	ta,	pos	ti	ta,	pos	ti	ta

44

BRACEO

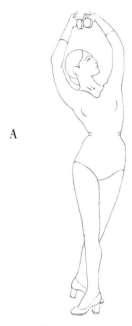

A

Fig. 1. *Braceo* IV

Bring R foot back into 1st on count of 4.

On the &, change to opposite position L:

        &   a   1   &   a   2   &   a   3   &   a   4
        Pos ti   ta, pos ti   ta, pos ti   ta, pos ti   ta

Bring L foot back into 1st on count of 4.

ON the &, change to opposite position R:

        &   a   1   &   a   2
        Pos ti   ta, pos ti   ta

Bring R foot back into 1st on count of 2.

On the &, change to L:

        &   a   3   &   a   4
        Pos ti   ta, pos ti   ta

Bring L foot back into 1st on count of 4.

Now change alternately on each &, four times:

        &   a   1   &   a   2   &   a   3   &   a   4
        Pos ti   ta, pos ti   ta, pos ti   ta, pos ti   ta

Braceo IV (B)

Position of body = face front
Feet = 4th as in *Braceo* IV (A)
Look = to R corner
Arms = in 1st, facing R (i.e., fingertips to R corner)
Note: L arm is across chest, making a curved but slightly downward slope from the shoulders, palms facing, elbows upheld.
Execute in exactly the same way as *Braceo* IV (A), except for the position of the arms.

Count:

           &   a   1   &   a   2   &   a   3   &   a   4
Castanets: Pos ti   ta,   pos ti   ta,   pos ti   ta,   pos ti   ta
On the &, quickly change position of arms through 1st to face 1st L, feet to L pointed in front.
Repeat to L, looking to R corner. Change position and repeat, change and repeat.

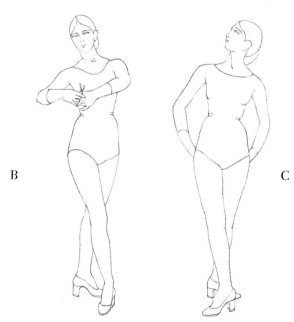

B   C

Figs. 2 & 3. *Braceo* IV

Braceo IV (C)

Position of body
Feet
Arms   } As Braceo IV (A)
Eyes

Execute four beats of A, quickly open arms outward through 2nd and downward to 5th behind at the same time. Change the position of feet, body, head and eyes to opposite side on:

     the &, *Postiseo*

Repeat 4 beats of A.

Change position, now bring arms forward to 1st R on:

     the &, *postiseo*

Execute 2 beats, change to 1st L on:

     the &, *postiseo*

Execute 2 beats, then change to 5th:

Count: &   a   1   &   a   3   Change to 5th
Castanets: Pos   ti   ta   pos   ti   ta
Change to 5th behind on & a 2 & a 4 Change to 5th behind

Braceo V

Position of body = face L corner
Feet = 3rd position
Look = to R corner
Arms = 5th behind

Count:

a 1	With R shoulder to R corner, incline body above the
Pos cop	waist to L, as Fig. 3 of *Braceo* IV (C)
a 2 a 3	Raise arms upwards through 2nd to 5th, as Fig. 1 of *Braceo* IV (A)
a 4	
Pos cop	
a 5 a 6	Down through 2nd to 5th behind, while bending to R and looking to L corner
a 1	
Pos cop	
a 2 a 3	Open arms forward into 1st R looking to R at hands
a	on *Postiseo*, as Fig. 2, *Braceo* IV (B)
Pos	

4	Take arms to 4th R *cop* looking to L corner on *cop*
cop	as Fig. 3 *Braceo* III
a 5 a 6	Move arms back to 5th behind
a 1	
Pos cop	
a 2 a 3	Forwards to 1st L looking to L at hands on *postiseo*
a	
Pos	
4	Take arms to 4th L *cop* looking to R on *cop*.
cop	
Repeat	

Count:

	a	1	a	2	a	3	a	4	a	5	a	6
Castanets:	Pos	cop	ta	riá	ta	riá,	pos	cop	ta	riá	ta	riá

Preparation for Braceo VI

Figs. 1 to 4 show the L arm held above the head making the outward circle of the wrist.

Figs. 5 to 8 show the same movement with both hands held above the head.

Finger and wrist exercise

Figs. 1, 2, 3 & 4. Preparation for *Braceo* VI

Exercise with two hands

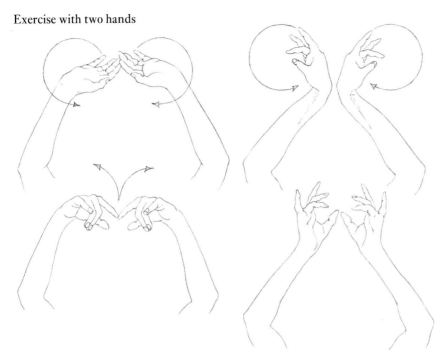

Figs. 5, 6, 7 & 8. Preparation for *Braceo* VI

Braceo VI (for fingers and wrists)

Position = face front
Feet = 4th, weight on L, R relaxed in front on ball of foot
Look = at working hand
Arms = L hand on hip (thumb at back, fingers stretched), R arm
      in 1st (palm outwards)
Movement = as soft, sinuous and flexible as possible

Count:	1 2 3 outwards	Without moving the arm, rotate the wrist by making outward circular movement with R hand, at the same time flexing fingers towards inner side of the wrist when circle is completed, stretch fingers to front
	4 5 6 inwards	Repeat circular movement inwards (i.e. fingertips inwards towards the body); complete circle back to original position

Practise several times with each hand, reversing position of body.

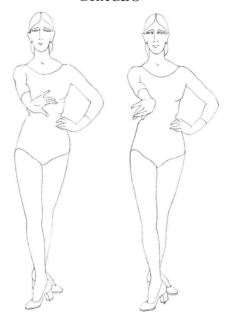

Figs. 1 & 2. *Braceo* VII

Braceo VII

Suitable music: *Soleares*

Position = face L corner

Feet = 4th, weight on L, R relaxed in front (*planta natural*)

Look = at working hand

Arms = L hand on hip, R arm in 1st (palm facing outwards towards L corner)

Movement = soft, sinuous and flexible

Count:

1 2 3 4 5 6 1 2 3   Execute 1½ bars of *Braceo* VI (9 beats)

              4   Bring back R foot and arm through 1st (facing front), changing weight on to R and turning body to face R with R hand on hip.

         5 6   Extending L arm and foot forward to R corner.

Repeat to alternate corners.

Fig. 3. *Braceo* VII   Fig. 1. *Braceo* VIII

Braceo VIII

Suitable music: *Soleares*
Position = face front
Feet = in 4th
Arms = 5th, palms outwards
Look = front, and natrually towards working arm on count 1 2 3,
       to front on 4 5 6

Count:

           Part 1

1 2 3   Circling outwardly with R arm through 2nd down-
           wards to 5th front, then upwards through 1st to 5th
           At the same time, make the circular movements with
           both wrists as explained in *Braceo* VI. The outward
           circle of the wrists should be completed when the work-
           ing arm is back in 5th

In this 5th position:

4 5 6   Make inward circle of the wrists

Repeat with L

Part 2

1 2 3   Now repeat the whole exercise, turning the wrists on count 1 (out) 2 (in) 3 (out)

4 5 6   in 5th, 4 5 6 (in)

Note: In Part 2, the wrist turns as the arm reaches the 2nd, 5th down and 5th, before making the final slower inward circle of the wrists on the count 4 5 6 (while the arms are held overhead).

Braceo IX

Suitable music: *Soleares*
Position = face front
Feet = 4th, weight on L, R *planta natural*
Look = front (away into distance)
Arms = L hand on hip, R in 5th (arm framing face, palm upwards facing ceiling)

Count: 1 2 3 4 5 6

With R hand execute $1\frac{1}{2}$ bars of *Braceo* VI

1 2 3   wrist makes outward circle

4 5 6   wrist makes inward circle

1 2 3   wrist makes outward circle

4 5 6   step forward on to R, bringing L 4th front

At the same time:

Arms change position through 1st with palms outwards to L in 5th and R on hip, while making the final inward circle with the wrist

Note: The object of this exercise is to attain maximum fluidity of fingers, wrist and arm movement, particularly when changing the position, as continuity of movement is essential. The body and shoulders should be relaxed, the chest expanded, back straight, weight down, head held high.

This exercise may be practised stepping forwards and backwards, also facing diagonally, i.e.:

R foot to L corner, in 4th position, R arm curved across chest (palm outwards). Change position as in *Braceo* VIII.

Fig. 1. *Braceo* IX   Figs. 1 & 2. *Braceo* X

Braceo X (with footwork)

Position = face front
Feet = 1st
Look = at working hand
Arms = 5th down in front

Count:

& a 1	Incline bodyweight on to ball of R foot in 4th front, at the same time raise R arm forwards and upwards to 5th (Fig. 1), while moving L hand to L hip, arm curved
& a 2 & a	Hold
3	Bring R foot and arms back to previous position
& a 4	Hold

Castanets: *ta*   ti   ti,   *ta*   ti   ti,   *ta*   ti   ti,   *ta*   ti   ti

Count:

&   a   1   &   a   2   &   a   3   &   a   4   &   a

BRACEO

Feet:	forward	hold	together	hold
Arms:	R 5th	hold	R lower	hold

Repeat with L. Execute four times, then:

Beginning with the R, take three walks forward, pause on fourth leaving L in front, weight on R. Beginning with L, three walks backwards, pause on fourth beat leaving R behind, weight on L.

Note: Move forwards with small steps, the weight directly under the body chiefly on the ball of the foot and carrying the weight forwards. Head and body erect, leaning from the waist slightly backwards, taking care to walk smoothly swinging the hips naturally. On the backward walk, incline slightly forwards.

Arms swing forwards and backwards naturally in opposition to working foot (i.e., L arm forward with R foot).

Count	*Castanets*	*Feet*	*Arms*
&			
a			
1	*ta*	Forward R	Swing L
&	ti		
a	ti		
2	*ta*	Forward L	R
&	ti		
a	ti		
3	*ta*	Forward R	L
&	ti		
a	ti		
4	*ta*	Point L	R
&	ti		
a	ti		
		3 beats to a walk	
1	*ta*	Back L	L
&	ti		
a	ti		
2	*ta*	Back R	R
&	ti		
a	ti		
3	*ta*	Back L	L
&	ti		
a	ti		

Count	Castanets	Feet	Arms
4	*ta*	Point R	R
&	ti		
a	ti		

Execute twice, then repeat the whole exercise from the beginning.

Castanets exercises to be used with Braceo I

Suggested music: Prelude (Albéniz) played slowly
In this exercise it takes 12 counts to make the circle. Practise with both the R and L arms, continue exercise counting in the same way *ad lib*.

Count: 6 beats to go down, 6 beats to go up.

    1   a   2   a   3   a   4   a   5   a   6   a
   ta ta, ti ti, ta ta, ti ti, ta ta, ti ti

Repeat *Braceo* I making three *golpes* to each count:

    1 & a   2 & a   3 & a   4 & a   5 & a
   ta ta ta, ti ti ti, ta ta ta, ti ti ti, ta ta ta

Repeat *Braceo* I with *caretilla*:

    1 a 2 a 3 a 4 a 5 a 6 a 1
   Ta,   riá,   riá,   riá,   riá,   riá,   riá

Repeat *Braceo* I with ta pi ta ta:

Slow *Zapateado* (music)

Count: 8, 4 down, 4 up.
1 & a 2 & a   3 &a 4 & a 5 & a6 & a 7 &a 8
ta pita *ta*, – –   pita pi *pi*, – –   ta pita *ta*, – –   pita pi *pi*
After 16 counts change to
& a 1 & a 2 & a 3 & a 4 & a 5 & a 6 & a 7 & a 8
tatapi,tatapi,tatapi,tatapi, etc.
After 8 counts change to
& a 1 & a 2 & a 3 & a 4 & a 5 & a 6 & a 7 & a 8
pipita,pipita,pipita,pipita, etc.

TACONEO AND ZAPATEADO

Zapateado is a technical feature of Andalusian dancing which involves the rhythmical beating of the feet on the ground.

Zapato means shoe.

Tacon = heel of the shoe.

Taconeo is the beating of the heels, while *Zapateado* is the use of the whole foot including the heels to make the sound.

Imagine your feet are hammers which, like the castanets, are going to beat a certain rhythm. In order to do this, one has to understand the quick changing of the weight of the body between the different types of beat. The important factor being the easy transference of weight from one foot to the other, or from one part of the foot to the other part to facilitate an even share of sound, particularly when the beats are very fast. The foot *must* fall relaxed using the weight of the leg from below the knee, or of the whole body if one stands on the foot.

The floor is struck by slightly flexing the knee. The beat is made by lifting the leg behind the body and letting the foot fall underneath. That is to say, the weight must always be directly under the body, but the beat is made from behind.

In the case of very quick beats, the foot is hardly raised at all though the principle is the same.

The wrong way is to raise the knee in front and stamp downwards with contracted muscles and a tense body. This natural and usual tendency needs to be avoided at all costs!

The tempo must always be maintained rhythmically, choosing the speed according to your ability to execute the steps. The clarity of sound should resemble a high-speed typist on a typewriter.

The exercises should always be practised to right and left. When possible, forwards and backwards, also – as progress is made these can be interchanged.

Taconeo and Zapateado – technical terminology

/ = change of foot
Ball = a beat with weight on ball of foot
Ball heel ⎤
Ball ⎬ = stand on ball of foot letting weight fall back on to heel
heel ⎦
Compas = bar of music
Double stamp = 2 stamps on same foot, changing weight on 2nd beat.
                Sometimes called flat stand
En place = on same place
Desplante = a rhythmic phrase used in *taconeo* to join or close
Flat = a stamp without changing weight or a stamp when the weight
    is evenly distributed between the feet. Example: Before mak-
    ing beats with the heels, while the ball of the foot remains
    on the ground
Golpe = beat
Heel/Heel = alternate heels (2 beats)
Heel heel = same foot (2 beats)
Heel ball ⎤
Heel ⎬ = standing on heel and letting weight fall forward on
ball ⎦   to ball (2 beats)
Knock = a beat striking the heel without changing weight
Planta = ball of foot
Planta natural = front foot relaxed on ball of foot in 4th front, weight
                on back foot
Stamp = a single beat with the whole foot, usually indicating change
      of weight
Stand* = used in 1st exercises instead of stamp to denote change of
      weight
Double stamp = two beats with the whole foot, changing weight on
           the second beat
Toe = tap toe tip

---

*In the early exercises the term stand is used instead of stamp, as it is essential
to remember change of weight; i.e. Flat stand = Double stamp.

TACONEO

See that your footwork is practised in the correct position. At first, you might find it easier to let the arms hang naturally at the side. If the hands are on the hips, be sure not to raise the shoulders.

Before trying Taconeo III, study the position again, and exercise *planta natural*. Remember that as you bring your foot from the 4th position into 1st, you should relax as you change your weight on to it, with a natural hip movement. Perfect this before attempting the double stamp. Hold skirt as instructed. A simple way to take hold of the skirt is to lift the knee sharply in front and catch the fold with thumb and first finger. If the arm is extended over the knee it will be in the right position to move to one side or the other. If the skirt is full enough, you should be able to bring it from the side in an imaginary circle, forward to the opposite side. The arms, though curved, should be held well away from the body. This enables the folds of the skirt to be seen to good advantage, so the circle should be as large as you can make it within the compass of the body. *Note:* Men should hold the front of the jacket, fingers curved inward over the diaphragm, with elbows held forward in line with the hips. It is wise to build on a solid technical foundation, so try to practise and understand each exercise before attempting the next one.

Introduce the more difficult exercises as you progress, but only very gradually, particularly the *Zapateado*, which is best left until the *Taconeo* is thoroughly mastered.

Taconeo I (single stamp – 1 beat)

Position of body = face front
Feet = in closed 1st (heels and toes together)
Hands = on hips (thumb at back)
With knees relaxed and close together, raise R foot behind, let it fall back into 1st (i.e., stand on it!) using the natural weight of the body to make a hammer-like beat as weight is transferred to R, finishing with the R foot on the ground, toes relaxed. Lift L and make a similar stamp. Practise slowly with alternate feet.

TACONEO

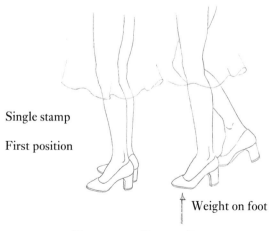

Single stamp

First position

Weight on foot

Figs. 1 & 2. *Taconeo* I

Count:

and a	Raise R foot behind
1 and a	Stand on R (stamp)
2 and a	Raise L behind
3 and a	Stand on L (stamp)
4 and a	Raise R.

Repeat *ad lib*.

Taconeo II (double stamp – 2 beats)

Suggested music: *Zapateado*

The difference between the flat and standing stamp is only a question of weight. The flat stamp is made in the same way as in *Taconeo* I, but without changing the weight. So a Double stamp is 2 beats made in exactly the same way with the same foot, but changing weight on the second beat.

Position = face front

Feet = together

Hands = on hips

Leaving weight on L, lift R foot behind, allow foot to relax back into 1st, flat, with heel and toes on the ground, the natural weight making the sound.

Repeat, this time changing weight on to R.
Repeat Double stamp with L.

Count:

and	Raise R behind	
a	flat R	
1	stamp R	= Double stamp
and	Raise L	
a	flat L	
2	stamp L	= Double stamp
and a	Repeat *ad lib.*, R R, L L, R R, L L, etc.	

Begin by practising very slowly; gradually quicken the pace when you can keep an even rhythm.

Taconeo III (see also Fig. on p. 39, *Planta Natural*)

Suggested music: *Zambra*

Position of body = face front
Feet = in 1st
Hands = on hips, shoulders relaxed
Make one flat and one stamping beat on R, point L in 4th front (relaxed on ball of foot – *planta natural*).
Repeat to L.

Count:

and	Raise R foot behind	
a	Flat R	
1	Stand R	=
2	Point L in 4th front	
a	hold	
3	hold	
	Brushing through 1st to	
4	raise L behind	Repeat to L
a	Flat L, etc.	and *ad lib*.

Now hold practice skirt with thumb and first finger of both hands, R arm in 2nd, L in 1st. Arms should be curved, with lifted elbows and shoulders held down. The arms move across the body to opposite position, the R arm coming forwards into 1st, and L to 2nd.

Count:

    & a 1   Arms move together to opposite position

    2 a 3   hold position

    4 a 1   change to opposite side

Now practise *Taconeo* III with arms and feet together.

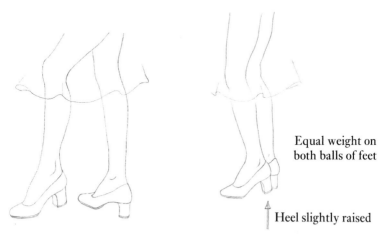

Equal weight on
both balls of feet

Heel slightly raised

Fig. 3. *Taconeo* III   Fig. 4. *Taconeo* IV

Taconeo IV

Suggested music: Zapateado

Feet = together
Knees = together relaxed
Hands = on hips
With the ball of the foot glued to the floor, raise L heel to make a single beat downwards. Repeat with alternate heels, starting slowly and gradually quickening the pace but keeping an even rhythm until you feel the thigh muscles aching (in fact, beginning to seize up!).
Now stop and relax.
Continue exercise, making 2 beats with alternate heels 8 times, then 3 beats, then back to single beats, *ad lib*.
In the same way, make the following:

Count:

    1 & a 2 & a 3 & a 4 & a 1 & a 2 & a 3 etc.
    L R L R R R R L R L L L L R L R R R R etc.

Note: Remember that the body must remain static during these exercises and ball of feet on the floor.

Now with the heels and knees together, raise both heels and strike downwards 8 times, then 8 double beats, and back again to alternate heels.

Taconeo V

Feet = together
Knees = together
Hands = on hips
This exercise is similar to *Taconeo* IV with an additional flat beat.
Flat L, raise R heel make a simple beat keeping ball of R foot on the ground; repeat with L heel in similar manner.
Repeat exercise to R, continue *ad lib*.
The sound of this exercise should be of continuous even heel beats of similar quality.
Remember the weight is evenly distributed between the feet during the heel beats. Accent the heel beats downwards to avoid a strong first beat followed by 2 weak ones.
En place:

Count:

1	L	flat
&	R	heel
a	L	heel
2	R	flat
&	L	heel
a	R	heel
3	L	flat
&	R	heel
a	L	heel

viz.: L/heel/heel, R/heel/heel . . .

First practise *Taconeo* V *en place*, then slowly moving backwards by placing the flat beat slightly behind the front foot (in closed 3rd position).

Only when an even sound is obtained should the speed be increased very gradually.

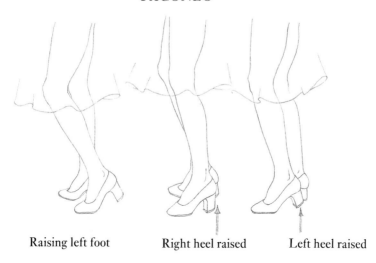

Raising left foot   Right heel raised   Left heel raised

Figs. 5, 6 & 7. *Taconeo* V

Up to now, wisely, you have probably raised the foot rather high behind your leg to make the flat and stamping beat. Now the time has come to make the same beat lower and smaller. Obviously the movement has to be small when the beats are quick.

If the beat is correctly made the sound will be sharp and clear. If it is a dull, thudding sound, you are probably tensing the muscles of your calves or clenching the toes. It is impossible either to make the correct sound or to keep an even rhythm if the feet are tense.

Taconeo VI

Suggested music: *Zapateado*

In this exercise the dancer travels forwards slightly with the feet in a closed 3rd position. One foot is only slightly in front of the other throughout.

You will notice the balance is mostly on the back foot, except on the stamp which subsequently comes on count a. Transfer the weight smoothly on to the front foot on this beat so that the change is not apparent. Remember the movement is made from below the knees. The dancer should travel forwards smoothly without any bobbing up and down while the heels make small even beats.

Count:

a	R	raise behind
1	R	stamp
&	L	flat
a	L	stamp
2	R	stamp
&	L	flat
a	L	stamp
3	R	stamp
&	L	flat
a	L	stamp
4	R	stamp
&	L	flat
a	L	stamp

Fig. 8. *Taconeo* VI

(viz. RLL, RLL, RLL, RLL)

Continue from 8 counts.

Repeat, starting with the L foot so that the R makes the flat, stamp (double stamp) in closed 3rd front.

Repeat with R and L for 4 counts, remembering to bring the front foot back into closed 1st to change feet.

= RLL, RLL, RLL, R (now bring L into 1st),

= LRR, LRR, LRR, L.

Taconeo VII

Redoble (doubling)

Position of body = face front

Feet = in closed 1st

Hands = on hips

The object of the following exercise is to get four distinct beats of crisp sound and equal value.

Remember to change the weight on the 3rd beat and to allow the weight of the body to be projected downwards to make the sound – do *not* try to force it by hitting the floor too hard, particularly with tension.

Redoble sencilla (simple):

Count:

1	L	stamp = 4 beats
2	R	flat
3	R	stamps
4	L	stamp

Practise 4 times, then repeat starting with R.
To make two or more *redobles* with the same foot, make the 4th beat a 'flat' instead of a stamping beat.

Count:

1	L	stamp = 4 beats
2	R	flat
3	R	stamp
4	L	flat

Practise 4 times with L and R.
The term 'double stamp' will now be used to denote 2 beats on the same foot.

Count:

a	R	Double stamp = 7 beats
1	R	
a	L	Double stamp
2	L	
a	R	Double stamp
3	R	
4	L	flat

Count:

a	L	Double stamp = 8 beats
1	L	
a	R	Double stamp
2	R	
a	L	Double stamp
3	L	
a	R	Double stamp
4	R	

Practise each sequence 4 times on R foot and 4 times on L without stopping, then alternate feet.

Cuatro tiempos = 4 beats (as *Redoble*)

Count:

	1	R	Stamp
&	a	L	Double stamp
	2	R	Stamp

Repeat starting with L.
Siete tiempos = 7 beats

Count:

&	1	R	Double stamp
&	2	L	Double stamp
&	3	R	Double stamp
	4	L	Stamp

Repeat starting with L.
Ocho tiempos = 8 beats

Count:

&	1	R	Double stamp
&	2	L	Double stamp
&	3	R	Double stamp
&	4	L	Double stamp

Repeat starting with L.
Variations on the last three exercises:

(a) *Cuatro tiempos:*   Practise 4 times on R & L
    Siete tiempos: Practise 4 times on R & L
    Ocho tiempos: Practise 4 times on R & L
    then alternately

(b) Cuatro tiempos: Practise 4 times on R & L
    Siete tiempos: Practise 4 times on R & L
    Ocho tiempos: Practise 4 times on R & L
    then practise (B)   3 times on R & L
        2 times on R & L
        1 time on R & L

Then repeat whole of last exercise in reverse starting
Ocho tiempos
Siete tiempos
Cuatro tiempos

Taconeo Desplante

Exercise for double stamps and stamp heel in 4th with accented beats.
F = in closed 1st then 4th

Count:

	and	R	stamp	
1 –	and	L	stamp heel	forward in 4th
a	*2*	R	double stamp	
	3	L	stamp	back, feet together
	4	R	stamp	
1 –	and	L	stamp heel	forward in 4th
a	*2*	R	double stamp	
	3	L	stamp	back, feet together
	4	R	stamp	
1 –	and	L	stamp heel	forward
a	*2*	R	double stamp	
3	and	L	stamp heel	stay forward
a	*4*	R	double stamp	
1 –	and	L	stamp heel	forward
a	*2*	R	double stamp	
	3	L	stamp	back, feet together
	4	R	stamp	

Foot slightly off ground

Taconeo Desplante – forward fourth

Repeat whole exercise with R forward in 4th.

Important: Repeat whole exercise with the accent on *and* which must be strong on the forward heel.

Taeoneo VII and *Taconeo Desplante* were arranged by Maestro Bautista of Barcelona, and given to Olga Valevska in 1936.

ZAPATEADO

Introduction to Zapateado I

It is comparatively easy to make clear beats with the heels providing there is no tension and that the weight is transferred without effort from one foot to the other. Now you have come to the exercises when you are going to use the ball of the foot as well as the heel. This is more difficult. You must be careful not to confuse the '*planta*' with the ballet position *demi pointe* (half point). The *planta* is literally the ball of the foot. When standing on the ball of the foot the heel is only slightly raised. The instep is not extended as in the *demi pointe* position when the heel and weight are drawn upwards as high as possible. You will remember that the weight must be relaxed downwards as you stand on the *planta*.

Try practising the following before attempting *Zapateado* I: To strengthen the *planta* beat, raise R foot underneath you, flexing ankle until the toe points up, then beat the floor with the ball of the foot without actually standing on it.

Count:

a   flex
1   beat   } practise slowly 8 times with R & L

then with a double beat, as follows

Count:

a   flex
1   beat beat
a   flex
2   beat beat
a   flex
3   beat beat

a flex
4 beat beat

Zapateado I

Suggested music: *Alegrías*
Begin as usual with feet together, working *en place* and remembering
to keep the weight directly under you.
Stand on ball of L
Let weight fall downwards on to L heel
Stamp on R

Weight forward

Weight on ball of foot ⟶

Left heel slightly raised off ground

Weight on left foot
Right foot raised to stamp

Figs. 9 & 10. *Zapateado* I – three beats

Position for beginning and end of *Zapateado* I

Fig. 11. *Zapateado* I

Count:

   and a L ball heel
    1 R stamp
   and a L ball heel
    2 R stamp

Repeat 8 times with L and R.

Now repeat taking a very small step forwards (quarter length of foot only) on to ball of L foot, let weight fall on heel, bring R foot to L on stamp:

Count:

   and a (forward) L ball heel
    1   R stamp (feet together)

   Repeat 8 times.

Repeat 8 times starting with R.
Practise progressing in a circle.

Zapateado I (A)

Suggested music: *Alegrías*

Stand on ball of L, let weight fall downwards on to L heel. Repeat slowly with alternate feet *en place*, then moving forwards, backwards and sideways, still keeping feet together.

Count:

   1 a   2 a   3 a
   ball heel ball heel ball heel

Now practise the following. You will notice the accented beat comes on alternate feet. This is important as it will help you to keep an even rhythm.

Count:

   1   &   a
   ball heel ball heel ball heel
   2   &   a
   ball heel ball heel ball heel
   3   &   a
   ball heel ball heel ball heel

When you can do this slowly, gradually quicken the pace, remembering that each beat must retain equal clarity and value.

Zapateado I (B)

Suggested music: *Zapateado Tipico* (Typical)

Count:

1	a	L ball heel
2	a	R ball heel
3		L stamp
4		R stamp

Repeat 4 times starting with L.
Repeat 4 times starting with R.
Then alternately, making the 4th beat a 'flat' instead of a stamp to free the working foot for the next sequence

Count:

1	a	R ball heel
2	a	L ball heel
3		R stamp
4		L 'flat'
5	a	L ball heel
6	a	R ball heel
7		L stamp
8		R 'flat'

Repeat 16 times slowly.
Repeat 16 times a little faster.

Zapateado II

Suggested music: *Zapateado Tipico*
Feet = together *en place*
Stand on ball of R, let weight fall on to R heel, flat with L – Repeat starting with L

Count:

&	R Ball)
a	R heel
1	L flat
&	L ball)
a	L heel
2	R flat

Fig. 12. *Zapateado* II

Right heel raised off ground
Weight on ball

Repeat the exercise stepping *slightly* forwards on ball of L foot, after making the L heel beat bring feet together on R flat beat. As you step forward (no more than quarter foot length), remember to keep your weight directly under you. Continue as above and so progress forwards, using alternate feet.

Now repeat the exercise making 2 flat beats.

Count:

        &   L ball
             L heel) 2 beats on the count &

        a   R flat

        1   R flat

        &   R ball
             R heel) 2 beats on the count &

        a   L flat

        2   L flat

Practise the exercise again progressing forwards but using the same foot. This will need a change of weight on counts 1 and 2.

Count:

        &   L ball
             L heel) 2 beats on the count &

        a   R flat

        1   R stamp

        &   L ball
             L heel) 2 beats on the count &

        a   R flat

        2   R stamp

Repeat with R.

Zapateado III 'Tres Tiempos'

Suggested music: *Zapateado Tipico*
In this exercise the knocking beat is introduced. It is made in exactly the same way as the 'flat' beat except that only the heel is used to make the sound. Strike the floor with the heel and lift the foot behind, ready for the next beat. Do not dig into the floor or leave the heel on the ground or raise the knee.

Position = face front
Feet   = together, execute *en place*

Count:

1	R ball ⟩
2	R heel
3	L knock
1	L ball ⟩
2	L heel
3	R knock

Right heel raised off ground
Weight on ball

Fig. 12. *Zapateado* II

Ballheel knock

Ball off ground →

Left foot raised off ground ready for ballheel

Figs. 13 & 14. *Zapateado* III

As in the previous exercise, this can be practised *en place* or walking forwards; in the latter case the 1st and 3rd beats will be placed *slightly* forwards, remembering to carry the weight over the feet.

Zapateado IV

Suggested music: *Zapateado Tipico*

So far you have learned how to make two separate beats on the same foot by standing on the ball of the foot and letting the weight fall strongly on to the heel. Now you are going to practise using the heel of the supporting foot to make a single beat by pressing on the ball of the supporting foot while lifting the heel to beat downwards, as in *Taconeo* IV and V.

Don't forget to change the weight on to the ball heel.

Note: You have to make two clear beats on the count

1, 2, 3, 4.

Remember to lift the foot after making the heel knocking beat. The feet are together, *en place* throughout.

Count:

1	L ball heel (weight remains on L)
&	R knock
a	L lift & beat heel (ball of L remains on ground)
2	R ball heel (weight remains on R)
&	L knock
a	R lift & beat heel (ball of R remains on ground)
3	
&	
a	Repeat as above, *ad lib.*
4	
&	
a	

Hold the back erect and avoid a bobbing movement, using the thigh muscles to raise the heels.

Zapateado V

Suggested music: *Zapateado Tipico*

Now you are going to make two heel beats on the same supporting foot. The second and third beat is made in the same way by lifting the heel and beating it downwards.

The feet and knees are together, relaxed. The weight centres downwards. The body should remain and appear static throughout.

Count:

1	L ball	
&	L heel	} 3 beats
a	L heel	
2	R ball	
&	R heel	} 3 beats
a	R heel	
3	L ball	
&	L heel	
a	L heel	} 4 beats
4	L heel	
&		
a		pause

Repeat with R.

Practise slowly 16 times, then repeat, gradually increasing the pace if you can keep an even sound.

Zapateado VI

Suggested music: *Zapateado Tipico*

Feet = together

In this exercise you make the opposite movement to ball heel, which is heel ball.

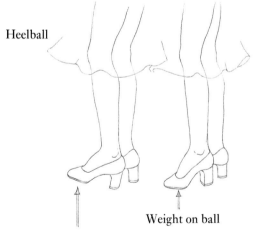

Heelball

Weight on ball

Ball off ground
Weight on heel

Figs. 15 & 16. *Zapateado* VI

75

Knock L heel, stand on L heel and allow the weight to fall forward on to ball of L foot. Repeat with alternate feet coming forwards.
The accent comes on the ball of the foot. Three even beats on each foot.

Count:

    & L knock heel
    a L stand on heel
    1 L allow weight to fall   } 3 beats
          forward on ball of L
    & R knock heel
    a R stand on heel
    2 R allow weight to fall   } 3 beats
          forward on ball of R

Zapateado VII

Suggested music: *Zapateado Típico*
Moving back slowly with feet together, make ball heel with alternate feet. You will notice that the accented beat also falls on alternate feet, but always on the ball of the foot, making two even beats on each foot.

Count:

    & L ball heel
    a R ball heel
    1
    L ball heel
    & R ball heel
    a L ball heel
    2 R ball heel
    &
    a
    3
    & } Repeat above *ad lib.*
    a
    4

Zapateado VIII

Suggested music: *Zapateado Típico*

You have practised a knocking beat with the heel in *Zapateado* IV – here you introduce a beat made by tapping the tip of the toe.

Up to now the *zapateado* exercises have been practised with the feet together or in a small closed 3rd, travelling forwards and backwards. In *Taconeo Desplante* you used the 4th position in front. In this exercise you use the 4th position behind. Bearing in mind that the feet should be correctly placed at all times, they should remain close together avoiding wide movements out of position. This mistake creates difficulty in transferring weight, as well as looking untidy, and causes loss of correct alignment with the rest of the body. The working knee is slightly turned out as the toe beats in 4th position.

STAMP WITH TOE TIP
Feet = together

Count:

1	R stamp
and	L tap toe tip (4th behind)
a	R heel (weight still on R)
2	L stamp

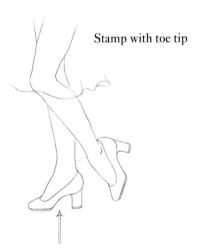

Stamp with toe tip

Flat on ground

Fig. 17. *Zapateado* VIII

and	R tap toe tip (4th behind)
a	L heel (weight still on L)
3	R stamp
and	
a	etc. Repeat *ad lib.*

DOUBLE STAMPS WITH TOE TIPS (9 SOUNDS)
Feet = together

Count:

1	R stamp
and	L tap toe tip (4th behind)
a	R heel (weight still on R)
2	L double stamp
and	R tap toe tip (4th behind)
a	L heel (weight still on L)
3	R double stamp
and	
a	etc.

Repeat *ad lib.*, continuing double stamps on each count with the accent on *a*, which will be the most difficult beat to sound clearly. Remember to hold the back straight and look ahead, not down at the feet, during practise – though the temptation may be great.

As you progress technically, there are passages in *zapateado* when the dancer deliberately looks down; not, however, in the early lessons.

Zapateado IX

Suggested music: *Zapateado Tipico*
Feet = together
Here you introduce a beat made by tapping the tip of the toe behind and knocking the heel in front. Step on ball of L foot, allow weight to fall on heel, tap tip of R toe in 4th behind (while standing on left), raise L heel to make beat on the count of 2, knock R heel in 4th front and again raise L heel to make the beat on 'a'. Repeat above with R.

So progressing forwards slowly, make an accented counter-rhythm with the heel of the foot upon which you step. You should travel forwards smoothly as in a walking movement, keeping the weight directly over the working foot and remembering to lift the foot

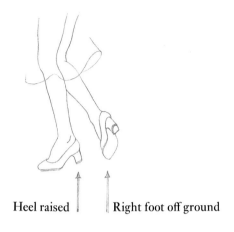

Heel raised | Right foot off ground

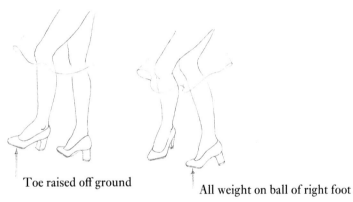

Toe raised off ground | All weight on ball of right foot

Figs. 18, 19 & 20. *Zapateado* IX

slightly after knocking either toe or heel.

Count:

1	L ball ⟩
&	L heel
a	R toe 4th behind
2	L heel (supporting leg)
&	R knock 4th in front
a	L heel (supporting leg)
3	R ball ⟩
&	R heel

79

a   L toe 4th behind
4   R heel (supporting leg)
&   L knock 4th in front
a   R heel (supporting leg)

Zapateado X

Suggested music: Slow *zapateado*
In the following exercise the toe tip is tapped in the 4th behind, in
the 2nd, and the heel in the 4th front, making a half circle forwards.
A *zapateado ronde de jambe en dedans* as it were! The movement is
made from below the knees, which are together when the toe makes
the tapping beat in the 2nd position, but the knee of the working
foot is turned out when the heel knocks in the 4th front and behind.

    Going forwards:

Count:

and 1	R ball heel	
and	L toe tip	4th behind
2	R heel	
and	L toe tip, knee turned in, 2nd position	
3	R heel	
and	L heel, knee turned out, 4th front	
4	R heel	

Side view

Showing toe in second position

Fig. 21. *Zapateado* X

Repeat with

A. In 1st position
   and 1 R ball heel
   and   L knock heel (1st)
    2 R heel
Repeat *ad lib.* alternate feet.

B.
   and 1 R D stamp
   and a L ball heel
    2 R stamp
Practise 8 times with R and L alternatively.

HEEL BALL HEEL ON SAME FOOT
C. Feet together   *En place*

Count:
    1 R stamp
  and a L ball heel
 2 and a R knock heel ball heel
    3 L toe tip   4th behind
   and R heel
    a L stamp

Note: Remember to put weight on to ball of R after knocking R heel.
Repeat, starting with L.

D.
   and R stamp
 1 and a L (knock) heel ball heel
 2 and a R (knock) heel ball heel
 3 and a L (knock) heel ball heel
 4 and a R (knock) heel ball heel
    5 L toe tip   4th behind
   and R heel
   a 6 L D stamp
    7 R toe tip   4th behind
   and L heel
   a 8 R D stamp
Repeat with L.

Zapateado XI

Suggested music: *Zapateado Tipico*

Face = front

Feet = in 4th position L front, working diagonally to L corner

Arms = Girls holding skirt as in Exercise 3, i.e. R arm in 2nd, L in 1st. Men holding jacket as before only slightly to R, away from working foot

Head = towards L corner

Eyes = looking downwards to L corner

In a small 4th position, with the R foot remaining behind throughout, execute the following:

Count:

1	R stamp	4th behind
a	L knock heel	4th front
2	L ball	
a	L heel	
3	R toe	4th behind
a	L heel	

Repeat whole exercise beginning with L, changing arms and direction to opposite position. Then repeat the whole exercise making a double beat on count 1.

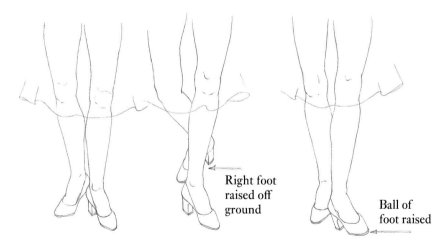

Right foot raised off ground

Ball of foot raised

Figs. 22, 23 & 24. *Zapateado* XI

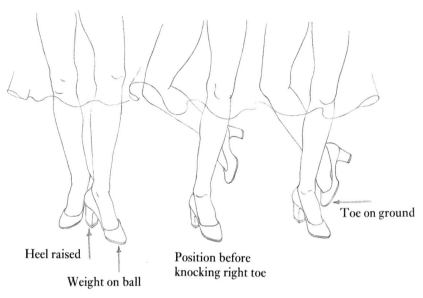

Heel raised

Weight on ball

Position before
knocking right toe

Toe on ground

Figs. 25, 26 & 27. *Zapateado* XI

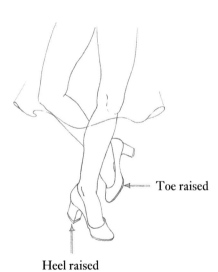

Toe raised

Heel raised

Fig. 28. *Zapateado* XI

Zapateado XII (*Compas* of 12 counts)

Suggested music: *Soleares*
Now you are going to combine *Zapateado* III, which takes you forwards, with *Zapateado* I, taking you backwards.
Do not try to cover too much ground.
6 *tres tiempos* forwards
15 *dos tiempos* backwards
During the *tres tiempos* the body is held erect and you should look as though you are walking naturally. On the *dos tiempos* a very slight inclination forwards of the whole body aids the balance on the backward movement.

Count:

1 and	R ball heel	
a	L knock	
2 and	L ball heel	forwards for 6 counts
a	R knock	

3 & a 4 & a 5 & a 6 & a

7	R ball heel	
and	L ball heel	backwards for 11 counts
a	R ball heel	

8 & a 9 & a 10 & a 11 & a

12	L flat stamp

Repeat the whole exercise beginning with L.

Zapateado XIII

Suggested music: *Alegrías*
Feet = together, with ball of L firmly on the ground throughout
The position of the feet on the 'flat' stamp which occurs on the counts 3, 6, 8, 10, 12, is in the direction of R diagonal 3rd, R heel moves forward to L instep, otherwise the exercise is practised with the feet together.

Count:

1 and	R ball heel	1st position
a	L heel	
2 and	R ball heel	
a	L heel	

84

3		R 'flat' stamp	diagonal 3rd
	a	L heel	
4		R ball heel	1st position
	a	L heel	
5 and		R ball heel	
	a	L heel	
6		R 'flat' stamp	diagonal 3rd
	a	L heel	
7 and		R ball heel	1st position
	a	L heel	
8		R 'flat' stamp	diagonal 3rd
	a	L heel	
9 and		R ball heel	1st position
	a	L heel	
10		R 'flat' stamp	diagonal 3rd
	a	L heel	
11 and		R ball heel	
	a	L heel	
12		R 'flat' stamp	diagonal 3rd

Repeat to L with L.

PREPARATORY EXERCISES IN CO-ORDINATION

Fandango

Music: *Slow Fandango*

So far you have learned how to practise some simple arm exercises, basic *taconeo*, *zapateado* and castanet rhythms. Now you are about to study a simple *fandango* step combined with arm movements and later with castanets.

Position = face front

Feet = 1st

Count:

1	R forward to 4th front, inclining weight on ball of slightly turned out foot
2, 3	Hold
1	R foot returns to 1st position
2, 3	Hold

Repeat with L and R *ad lib*.

The feet should move smoothly forwards and together in a sinuous, relaxed manner, as the weight is changed the hips move naturally.

Now repeat the exercise using the same arm as the working leg, i.e. R arm comes down as R leg comes forward.

Count	Castanets	Feet	Arms
1	*cop*	forward R from 5th	R makes outward
2	hold	hold	circle to
3	hold	hold	5th down
1	*cop*	R returns to 1st	R continues to
2	hold	hold	move upwards
3	hold	hold	through 1st to 5th

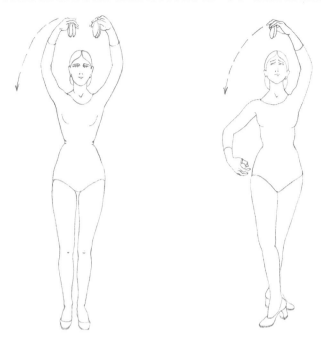

Figs. 1 & 2. *Fandango* exercise

Paso de Vasco
(Small *Pas de Basque en place*)

FEET

Position = face front, looking front
Feet = 1st
Arms = 5th

Count:
1   Step R with R to small 2nd
2   Step L into 3rd front ⎫
3   Mark R in 3rd behind ⎬ *En place*

Repeat L, on alternate feet 16 times, then repeat with the arm movements.
The head looks to L corner as the R foot moves into 2nd and the L arm begins an outward circle, reaching 5th down on the 2nd count and completing circle to 5th on the third count.

Figs. 3, 4, 5 & 6. *Pas de Basque*

The movements of both feet and arms should be smooth and continuous, taking care to pass through all positions correctly.

ARMS

Count:

1	L begins outwards circle, look L
2	L reaches 5th down, look front
3	L completes upward circle to 5th
1	R begins outward circle, look R
2	R reaches 5th down, look front
3	R completes upward circle to 5th

Count	Castanets	Feet	Arms
1	ta	step R	L
a	ti		
2	ta	step 3rd front L	L 5th down

a	ti		
3	ta	mark R 3rd behind	L 5th
a	ti		
1	ta	L	R
a	ti		
2	ta	R	R 5th down
a	ti		
3	ta	L	R 5th
a	ti		

Exercise for Malagueña

FEET

Music: *Malagueña*

Position = face to front
Look = to front
Feet = in 1st
Arms = in 5th
Hop and point R and L in front. Repeat.

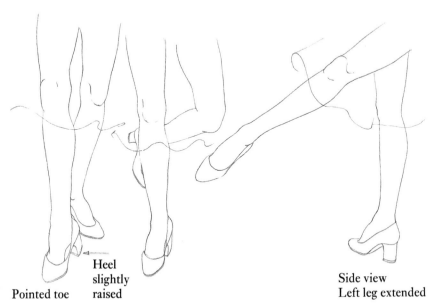

Pointed toe   Heel slightly raised   Side view
Left leg extended

Figs. 7, 8 & 9. Exercises for *Malagueña*

Then bend L knee and kick L leg forwards.

Repeat to other side, beginning with L.

This easy hopping step is made with the back held straight, toes pointed and the knee stretched on the kick.

    Note: No castanet rhythms will be given during the following eight exercises. When the latter are perfected a simple rhythm of your own choice may be useful. The type of music is only suggested where it is thought to be helpful.

ARMS

Held in 5th throughout.

Count	Castanets	Feet	Arms
1	ta	hop L, point R	Held in 5th throughout
a	ri		
2	á	hop R, point L	
a	ri		
3	á	hop L, point R	
a	pi		
4	ta	hop R, point L	
a	ri		
5	á	hop R, bend L	
a	ri		
6	á	hop R, kick L	
a	pi		
1	ta	hop R, point L, etc.	

Cortados
(*Coupé* or cutting step)

One foot cuts the other away and takes its place.

Position = face front

Feet = 3rd R front

FEET

Count:

    a   Raise L foot behind to reach mid-calf, knee turned out and toe pointed down. Keeping close to supporting leg

Figs. 10 & 11. *Coupé*

1	let it fall back into 3rd behind and stand on it as R foot
a	cuts the front of supporting leg in a similar manner
2	Repeat the cutting step by standing on the R foot as
a	the L cuts the back of supporting leg as above
3 a 4	Repeat *ad lib.*
etc.	

The cutting step is executed *en place.*
Look = Diagonal R.
Arms 4th position L up

Destaque (*battement*)

Feet = 3rd position, R behind
Arms = 4th, L up
Destaque is done in the same way as *grande battement* in ballet.
Usually it is from the 3rd position to either the 4th front or 2nd
position – often a diagonal 2nd is used, as in this exercise.

Fig. 12. *Desaque*

Slide the R foot through *pointe tendue* to R diagonal 2nd, raising the R foot as high as possible while holding the back erect and keeping both knees stretched and pointing the toe – still controlling the upward beating movement close into 3rd front.

Count:

a	Slide R to diagonal 2nd
1	close in 3rd front
a	Slide R to diagonal 2nd
2	close in 3rd behind
a	Slide R to diagonal 2nd
3	close in 3rd front
4	Change the arms to 4th R up (L moves through 1st downwards as the R moves upwards)

Repeat all to L.

Cuña
(Rocking or swinging step)

Position = face front
Feet = together
Arms = in 4th, L up
Cross R foot over L, holding the ankles together, standing on the half-toe with the weight equally divided, make a rocking movement *en place* changing the weight from the ball of one foot to the other, while the ankles swing from side to side and the feet remain in place.

Count:
1   cross R over L
2   rock to L
3   rock to R

Repeat rocking movement 6 times, then change to L in front. A similar step is to cross the R foot over the L in *demi plié*; alternately raise the R heel and let it fall in the same place while raising the L heel without moving the ball of the foot.

Count:
1   cross R over L
2   raise R heel and let it fall, while simultaneously
3   raise L heel without moving ball of foot

Repeat as above with R in front 6 times, then repeat with L.
   Note: These steps can also be practised turning in place.

Lizadas
(*Glissade* or gliding step)

Position = face front
Feet = in 3rd position, R in front
Arms = in 4th, L up
This gliding step is made in almost the same way as the balletic *glissade*, except that usually the movement is smoother and smaller.

   In *demi plié*, extending the instep, slide the ball of the R foot into a small 2nd position, stand on the R foot and slide the L foot into the 3rd behind.

Count:

	a	Slide R into small 2nd
	1	bring L into 3rd behind
2	3	hold
1	2	hold
	3	slide L into small 2nd
	1	slide R into 3rd in front
2	3	hold
1	2	hold
	3	slide R into small 2nd
	1	slide L into 3rd front
2	3	hold
1	2	hold
	3	slide L into small 2nd
	1	slide R into 3rd front
2	3	hold

⎰ *glissade changé*
⎱ changing positions of feet in 3rd

Echado

(*Jeté* or throwing step)

Position = face front
Feet = in 3rd position, R front
Arms = in 5th down

Count:

&	*Demi plié* on both feet
a	Slide R foot to 2nd position
1	spring off the L foot and land on the R foot with bent knee in position vacated by L. As the R foot reaches the ground, raise the L foot (with the toe pointed downwards and the knee turned out) behind calf of R leg (as in Fig. 19)
& a 2	Repeat to L with L and alternately with R and L 8 times.
etc.	There should be no pause between the steps. The *demi plié* is used to begin the step but is omitted after the first *echado* or *jeté* is made, since the supporting leg is already bent.

94

Cambios
(*Changement de pied* or changes)

Look = front
Arms = 5th down
Feet = 3rd, R in front
Changes in 3rd position (*demi plié*)
Half bend the knees, keeping heels on the ground, spring into the air. Simultaneously, change the feet, landing in 3rd with L in front in *demi plié*

Practise 8 times, taking care to hold the back straight, point the toes in the air and land smoothly with bent knees.

Count:

&	half bend knees in 3rd
a	Spring and change feet
1	landing with bent knees in 3rd with R behind
&	Repeat as above alternately
a	changing feet and
2	landing on each count
etc.	

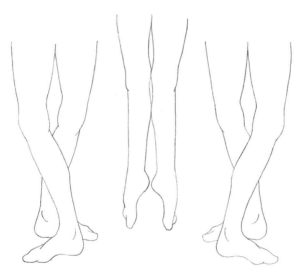

Figs. 13, 14 & 15. *Cambios*

Sequence of Cortados y Cambios
(Cuts and changes/*Coupé changements*)

Position = face front
Feet = 3rd, R front
Arms = 4th, L up
Execute 8 cuts, starting with back foot.
Execute 7 changes.

Count:
    a   Raise back foot
    1   stand on back foot and raise front foot.

Repeat whole exercise, starting the cuts with the R in 3rd behind, arms 4th, R up.

Count	Feet	Count	Feet
a	raise L foot	. . . a	hold
1	stand L, raise R	5	L
a	hold	a	hold
2	R	6	R
a	hold	a	hold
3	L	7	L
a	hold	a	hold
4	R . . .	8	R

As Fig. 10

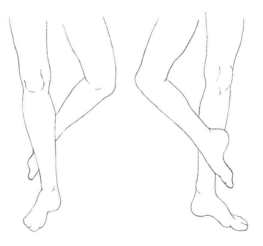

As Fig. 11

Cortado

PREPARATORY EXERCISES IN CO-ORDINATION

Count	Feet	Count	Feet
a	hold	a	demi plié
1	Close L 3rd back	5	change . . .
a	demi plié	a	alternately
2	change	6	to count of 8
a	demi plié	a	
3	change	7	
a	demi plié	a	
4	change . . .	8	

Note: Some of the figures are drawn without shoes for clarity, also because *zapatillas* are worn in many classical and regional dances.

ARMS

Count:
<blockquote>

a 1 to 8   In 4th, L up, look diagonal R

a 1 to 8   In 5th, hold for changes
</blockquote>

Emboteados
(*Retirer*)

Music: *Pasodoble*

Rhythm = *Passodoble*
Position = face front
Feet = 3rd, R front
Arms = 5th

FEET

Raise R foot in front to reach mid-calf, keeping close to the supporting leg, with knee turned out and toe pointed down. Cut to the calf of supporting back leg and step hop with R into 3rd behind, releasing the L foot, which is now in front, to repeat the same movement with L as above.

The direction is travelling backwards.

97

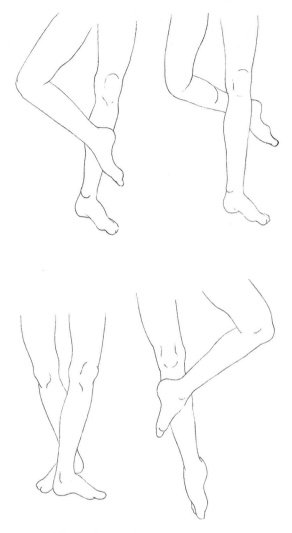

Figs. 16, 17, 18 & 19. *Emboteados*

Count:
    a   Raise R in front
    1   step R in 5th behind
    a   hop R and raise L
    2   step L in 3rd behind

Repeat 16 times.
Practise the feet before using the arms.

ARMS

The arms make the same movement as in *Braceo* I, beginning with the R. It takes four counts on the outward circle to reach the 5th down and four counts up to reach the 5th. Each arm must move smoothly all the time and reach the 5th position exactly on the count of eight.

Punta y Talon y Dos Emboteados
(Toe, heel and two *retirés*)

Music: *Seguidilla Manchegas*

Position = face front
Feet = 3rd, R front
Arms = 5th

FEET

Count:

1 a 2	Step on L *en place*, tap R toe tip in diagonal 2nd with
a	knee bent and turned in.
3	Tap R heel in same spot with knee still bent but turned
a	out,
4	then place ball of R foot in 3rd front (leaving weight
a	on L) ready to make

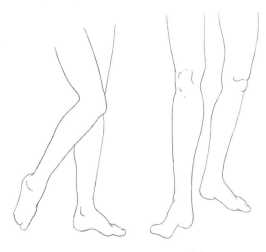

Figs. 20 & 21. *Punta y Talon*

99

5 a 6   one retiré back with R and one retiré with L.
   a

Repeat all to L.

Remember to lift the foot slightly before making both the toe and the heel step, which should be small, neat and underneath the body. In musical terms, the movement is staccato. Now repeat the whole exercise hopping on each foot except for the count 1.

Look at working foot on toe, heel and at audience on the *retirés*.

ARMS (as in *Braceo* I)

Count:

1   Arms in 5th (it takes six counts to complete the outward circle)

2   R arm reaches 2nd

3   R arm reaches 5th down

4   R arm reaches
                  1st
5   R arm reaches

6   R arm reaches 5th

Repeat with L.

A steady movement is essential when passing through all the positions

Count	Castanets	Feet	Arms
			5th
1	ta	step on L	R makes outward circle
a	ri		
2	á	tap R toe	and
a	ri		
3	á	tap R heel	reaches 5th down
a	pi		
4	ta	R in 3rd front	
a	ri		
5	á	retiré R	
a	ri		
6	a	retiré L	reaches 5th
a	pi		

Lazos
(Chains)

Music: *Seguidilla*
This exercise has a certain affinity with the Charleston, but the movement in *Lazos* is very small and smooth, hardly raising the feet off the ground. The alternate changing of the feet is done by rotating the whole leg from the hip, in and out, with relaxed knees.
Position = face front
Feet = in 5th, half toe (*demi pointe*)
Arms = 5th down

FEET

Stand on ball of both feet, R front in 5th (i.e. feet close together, knees turned out).

Count:

    a   with weight on front foot, turn both legs in, knees locked, at the same time

    1   Bring L into 5th front, transferring weight on to L as both legs turn out.

        Continue travelling forwards with alternate feet 12 times,

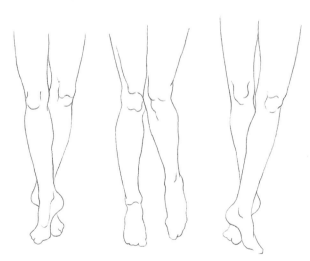

Figs. 22, 23 & 24. *Lazos*

then in reverse, starting with the front foot and placing it in the 5th behind, so travelling backwards.

Transfer the weight smoothly; the movement should be continuous, small and neat.

Note: Both heels turn outward when knees are locked during changes of weight.

ARMS

Feet going forwards.

Count:

| a | I | a | 2 | a | 3 | a | 4 | a | 5 | a | 6 |

Gradually raise arms from 5th down outward to 2nd

| a | I | a | 2 | a | 3 | a | 4 | a | 5 | a | 6 |

continue the upward and outward circle to 5th

Feet going backwards.

| a | I | a | 2 | a | 3 | a | 4 | a | 5 | a | 6 |

Gradually move the arms from 5th outwards and downwards through 2nd.

| a | I | a | 2 | a | 3 | a | 4 | a | 5 | a | 6 |

Continue the downward circle to 5th down.

Note: There is no pause; the arms should make a slow, continuous movement.

Count	Castanets	Feet	Arms
a		turn knees in	arms move
I	ta	forward R knees out	slowly
a	ti	turn knees in	upwards and
2	ta	forward L out	outwards from
a	ti	in	5th (down)
3	ta	R out	taking
a	ti	in	12 counts
4	ta	L out	to reach
a	ti	in	5th
5	ta	R out	
a	ti	in	
6	ta	L out	
a	ti	in, etc	

Repeat travelling backwards for 12 counts, taking the R foot back on the count 1.

The arms move outwards and downwards to 5th (down), taking 12 counts.

Campanelas or Simple Rodazan
(Circling the leg) (*rond de jambe*)

Music: *Pasodoble*
Note: An easy way to practise this exercise is to replace the *Rodazan* on count 4 by pointing the foot on the ground in diagonal 2nd.
When you have perfected the co-ordination of arms and feet you can then concentrate on making the actual circle in the air.
Position = face front
Feet = 3rd, R front
Arms = 5th

Figs. 25 & 26. *Rodazan (Campanelas)*

FEET

Count:

1 Keeping weight underneath,
   step into very small 2nd with R as body makes a quarter
   turn to R

2 L describes a small inward circle on the ground and passes
   in front of the R into 4th position front (the positions of
   body and feet facing sideways to audience, *Rond de jambe*
   and quarter turn to R)

3 Cut with R to face audience, lift and hold L thigh with bent
   knee facing diagonal L, at the same time describe an outward

4 circle in the air with the lower leg, taking care not to drop
   the thigh (*Rond de jambe en l'air*). Akin to similar movement
   in the French *Can Can*, but making one circle of the leg
   only.

   Repeat all to L.

Figs. 27 & 28. *Rodazan (Campanelas)*

ARMS

Count:
- 1   L arm makes outward circle to
- 2   4th front as body turns R
  Look at audience, keeping R arm well behind head as body turns sideways
- 3   Hold position
- 4   L arm completes circle to 5th, body faces front

The arms and feet move smoothly and continuously throughout. The rather sharp *Rodazan* on count 4 should make the skirt fly upwards.

Count	Castanets	Feet	Arms
1	ta	step R	with R remaining up, L
&	ta		makes outward circle to
a	ri		4th position
2	á	L to 4th	
&	ta		hold
a	ri		hold
3	á	*Coupé* R	hold
&	ta		L continues
a	ri		upward circle
4	á	*Rodazan* L	to 5th
&	ta, etc.		Hold

Repeat all to L.

Vuelta por Delante, por Detras y Vuelta Normal
(Forward turn, backward turn and ordinary turn)

Music: *Malagueña*
Position = face front
Feet   = 3rd, R front
Arms = 4th, L up

PREPARATORY EXERCISES IN CO-ORDINATION

FEET

VUELTA POR DELANTE

Count:

    1   Moving to R, step into small 2nd with R

    2   Cross L over R and stand with the weight equally divided

    3   Turn R on balls of feet, finishing the turn facing front with weight on L, R in front in *planta natural*. (Begin to change weight on to L as the body faces the back.)

Take small steps, keeping the weight directly underneath the body. The turn and transference of weight should be made smoothly without any rising up or down. In balletic terms, no relevé.

Practise 4 times to R and L.

VUELTA POR DETRAS

Technically, the *vuelta por detras* is made in the same way as *por delante*, except the direction is reversed. The L foot crosses behind the R, so the turn is therefore made to the L and the L foot finishes in front.

    Practise as above.

VUELTA NORMAL

Vuelta normal is made in a similar manner as *vuelta por delante*, but finishes as it begins, with feet in the 3rd position, R front.

ARMS AND HEAD

VUELTA POR DELANTE

Count:

    1   Arms move from 4th, L up, to 2nd (L moves downwards as R moves sideways). Look front

    2   Change to 4th, R up. Still look front

    3   On turn, change through 1st to 4th, L up

Quickly turn head R to look front again

The movement of the arms and feet must co-ordinate throughout. The head movement controls the turn.

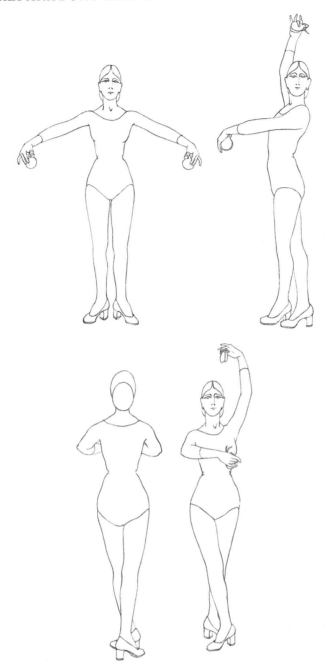

Figs. 29, 30, 31 & 32. *Vuelta por Delante. Vuelta Normal*

VUELTA POR DETRAS

At first, the same arm movement as above can be practised. When this is perfected, try the following:

Count:

1 Arms move from 4th, L up, to 2nd. Look front
2 Change back to 4th, L up. Look front
3 On the turn, change arms through 1st to 4th, R up

Quickly turn head to L and finish looking front

VUELTA NORMAL

As for *Vuelta por delante.*

FORWARD TURN

Count	Castanets	Feet	Arms
1	ta	step R	from 4th to 2nd
á	ri		
2	á	cross L over R	to 4th, R up,
a	ri		through 1st
3	á	turn R	to 4th, L up
a	pi	R, *planta natural*	hold

Malagueña (Exercise 2)
Music: *Malagueña*

Stepping in a large circle, holding the arms in 4th down, R front, take three steps forward.

Count:

1 2 3 R, L, R, stepping on the ball of the foot in a natural, graceful movement, slightly swinging the hips
4 one *vuelta por delante* crossing L over R
5 turning to R
6 finishing turn, weight on L foot, R in *planta natural*

You are now in the correct position to repeat the three steps forward with the R foot commencing.

Repeat the whole exercise in a circle round the studio. All the movements are smooth and elegant in style, with the head held high, looking in the direction towards which you are travelling.

ARMS

Count:

1 2 3	Hold in 4th down, R front
4 5	L arm changes to 4th down, L front, and
6	changes back to R front

Note: As the L foot crosses the R to make the *vuelta*, the L arm moves forward to 4th down, L front, and changes back to R in front as the turn finishes. Remember to hold up the elbows and to keep the arms curved.

Leave the head momentarily behind on the turn.

Count	Castanets	Feet	Arms
1	ta,	walk R	4th down, R front
a	ri		hold
2	á,	walk L	hold
a	ri		hold
3	á,	walk R	hold
a	pi		hold
4	ta,	cross L over R	change to L front
a	ri		
5	á,	turn R	
a	ri		
6	á,	*planta natural,*	change to R front
a	pi	R in front	

Vuelta de paso
(Simple turning exercise)

Rhythm: *Pasodoble*
Position = face front, with the back held straight throughout
Feet = 3rd, R front
Arms = 4th down, R front

FEET

Count:

1	Looking to R, step R into small 2nd.
	Continuing in the same direction

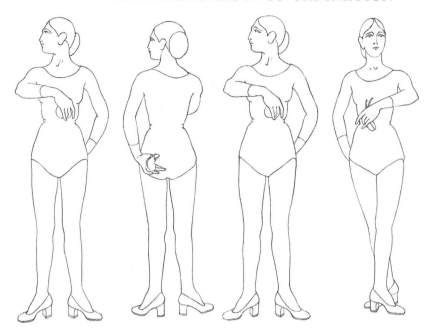

Figs. 33, 34, 35 & 36. *Vuelta de Paso*

2   Step L into 2nd (making ½ turn to R, finish with back to the audience)

3   Continue stepping the same way on to R in 2nd, completing turn to R. Weight equally divided between the feet throughout

4   Finish pointing L in 4th front, *planta natural*, or in 5th

HEAD MOVEMENT

Look towards the direction in which you are travelling. Hold the head *still* as the body makes the first ½ turn, then turn head as quickly as possible in the same direction on final ½ turn.

Look to front on *planta natural*.

Note: Look at a definite object at eye level and remember that the correct head movement in co-ordination with the body dictates the quality of the turn, particularly in a series of quick turns (*petits tours*).

ARMS

Count:

I 2 3	The arms remain in the 4th (down), R front
4	Change to reverse arms as foot is pointed in 4th front

The arms should not be used to assist the turn, but should remain relaxed throughout.

The important factor in executing the turn is the correct head movement. When travelling to the R, think of quickly bringing round the L shoulder and the whole body on count 2, followed by the quick turn of the head on count 3.

	Count	*Castanets*	*Feet*	*Arms*
look R	I	ta,	travelling to R, R in 2nd	4th down
hold	&	ta		R front
hold	a	ri		hold
hold	2	á,	L in 2nd	hold
	&	ta		hold
	a	ri		hold
turn and	3	á,	R in 2nd	hold
look R	&	ta		hold
	a	ri		hold
look front	4	á,	Point L, 4th front	4th down, L front
	&	ta		hold
	a	ri		hold
	I	á,		hold

Repeat all to L.

Peteneras with turn *in place*
(Popular Andalusian step)

Music: *Peteneras*
Position = face front; look front and over R shoulder on the turn
Feet = 3rd, L front
Arms = 4th R up
Direction = travelling to R, then turning in place to R

Figs. 37, 38, 39 & 40. *Petenera*

FEET

Count:
1   Step small 2nd with R
2   Point L tip of toe in 4th front, in the same position raise the knee, turned out
3   Stand on L in 4th front
     Repeat 4 times to R and 4 times turning in place

HOW TO MAKE THE TURN

On the last beat of fourth *Petenera*, instead of standing on the L in 4th front,

3 1   make 1 *golpe* in 1st with L, before standing on L and continuing the same *Petenera* step, this time making a ¼ turn in place to R on each of 3 beats. The L foot acts as a pivot as the body turns facing the side, back, side and

112

front to complete one full turn. You are then in position to repeat the whole sequence to the L.

Remember to hold the back erect and look over the R shoulder, which should lead the turning *Petenera* in place.

Repeat whole sequence to L and *ad lib*.

ARMS

The arms are held in the 4th position with the R arm framing the face, until they gracefully change in front, through 1st, to reverse 4th position, as the weight is changed on to the L foot after the *golpe*, when the body faces the side to make the first $\frac{1}{4}$ turn.

1st, 2nd and 3rd *Peteneras*:

Count	Castanets	Feet	Arms
1	ta	step R	4th, R up
2	riá	point and lift L	hold
3	riá pi	stand on L	hold

4th *Petenera*:

1	ta	step R	hold
2	riá	point and lift L	hold
3	riá pi	*golpe* L, feet together	hold

5th, 6th, 7th & 8th *Peteneras* (make $\frac{1}{4}$ turn 4 times in all):

1	ta	stand L	change to 4th, L up
2	riá	point R	hold
3	riá pi	stand L	hold

Sostenidos
(Sustained step)

Music: *El Vito*
Position = face front
Feet = 3rd, R front
Arms = 4th, L up

Figs. 41, 42, 43, 44, 45 & 46. *Sostenidos*

PREPARATORY EXERCISES IN CO-ORDINATION

FEET

Count:

1 2	
3	Mark on ball of R in 3rd front, extend and
1 2	Mark on ball of R in 2nd
3	Repeat as above
1 2	Repeat as above
3	Repeat as above
1	Step on R in small 2nd, travelling sideways
2	Step on L in 3rd behind ⎫ small *pas de*
3	Step to 2nd with R ⎬ *bourré changé*
1 2	Bring L into 3rd front
3	Repeat *Sostenidos* to L with L

Remember that the knees are relaxed and that the *pas de bourré changé* is a natural step on the ball of the foot without any *relevé* or rising on the half toe. You will notice the step begins on the last beat of the previous bar of music. This is a characteristic of many Spanish steps.

Look over R shoulder to working foot.

ARMS

Count:

1 2	
3	The arms remain in 4th on marking step
1 2 3	*Sostenidos*
1 2 3	*Sostenidos*
1 2 3	On *pas de bourré* the arms change to the reverse position, the L arm moves inwards as the R moves outwards through the 2nd to the 4th, R up
	Look at audience on *pas de bourré*
1 2 3	Hold

Repeat to L.

Count	Castanets	Feet		Arms
1				
2				
3		mark R in 3rd		4th, L up

Count	Castanets	Feet		Arms
a		hold		hold
1	ta	mark R in 2nd		hold
2	riá	hold		hold
3	riá	mark R in 3rd		hold
a	pi	hold		hold
1	ta	mark R in 2nd		hold
2	riá	hold		hold
3	riá	mark R in 3rd		hold
a	pi	hold		hold
1	ta	step R	*Pas de bourré*	Change to
2	riá	step L		4th, R up
3	riá	step R		hold
a	pi			hold
1	ta	close L, 3rd front		hold
2	riá	hold		hold
3	riá	mark L in 3rd on		hold
a	pi	repeat to L		hold

Escobilla
(Brushing step)

Music: *El Vito*
Position = face front
Feet = 3rd, L front
Arms = in 5th
Dancing in diagonal line to L corner, with the working foot slightly turned out.

Count:

1 2 3		Step on L, brush and point R through 1st into 4th front	
1 2		Step on R in 4th	
	3	progressing forwards, brush L in 4th front and point	
1		Take a very small step forwards on L and face sideways (L shoulder to audience)	
	2	Bring feet together	
	3	Step upstage with R	
1		Step L 4th front	Small *Pas de*
	2	Step R very small 2nd	*Bourré changé*
	3	Step L 3rd behind	almost in place

116

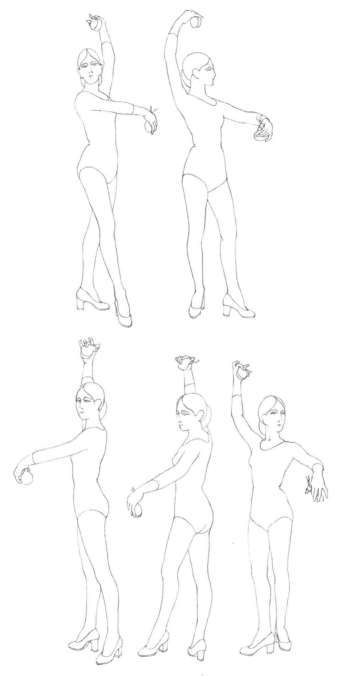

Figs. 47, 48, 49, 50 & 51. *Escobilla*

PREPARATORY EXERCISES IN CO-ORDINATION

Repeat all to R and again to L.

Count	Castanets	Feet	Arms
1	ta	in a diagonal line, step L	in 4th, L overhead
2	ta	in a diagonal line, brush R	hold
3	riá	in a diagonal line, point R	hold
1	ta	in a diagonal line, step R	change inwards
2	ta	in a diagonal line, brush R	to 4th
3	riá	in a diagonal line, point L	R overhead
1	ta	step on L	in 5th
2	postiseo	bring feet together	in 5th
3	cop	step back on R	in 5th
1	ta	step on L, 3rd front	L moves
2	riá	step on R, small 2nd	inwards to
3	riá pi	step on L, 3rd behind	4th, R up (hold for next 3 beats)

Repeat to R and L.

ARMS

Count:

1 2 3	4th position, L overhead, in diagonal line to L corner
1 2 3	Change inwards to R overhead, through 1st
1 2	Bring to 5th
3	Hold
1 2 3	L arm moves inwards. The position is now 4th with R overhead
1 2 3	Hold, then repeat as above

Repeat.

The arms should move smoothly and gracefully from one position to the next. In the diagonal 4th, remember to hold the arm well behind the head, with the front arm curved across the chest, so that a straight diagonal line is made with the pointing foot.

Look at the audience on the first bar of *escobilla* (3 beats), then towards the direction in which you are travelling on the second bar; look back to the audience on the third and fourth bars of music, dropping the eyes on the *Pas de bourré*, during which the small movement should make the skirt swirl in a figure of eight.

Practise feet, arms and castanets separately, then feet and arms together, then feet and castanets together.

Lastly, when you have mastered all separately, try all three together.

Exercise for Vuelta de Pecho

Position = face wall
Feet = L crossed over R (weight equally divided, toes face front)
Body = inclining forwards from the waist, but only slightly to begin with
Arms = R hand crossed over L, fingertips against the wall at about shoulder level.

Gradually aim to keep the crown of the head facing the wall all the time, but this requires great flexibility of the back and should, therefore, be practised with the utmost care.

Turn R, making a complete circle from the waist, during which you will bend backwards as you face outwards towards the centre of the room. Continue turn circling from the waist until you face the wall again. The fingers pressing against the wall are in order and steady the upper part of the body.

The turn begins from below the waist, followed by the shoulders which continue the movement before the supporting lower part of the body completes the circle, in a corkscrew motion.

This bend should be practised very gradually and gently. Start by putting the fingers fairly high on the wall, hardly bending at all.

Practise both ways to L and R, but only a few times.

The preparation for this turn is the same as for *vuelta normal*, with the additional corkscrew movement of the upper torso.

Vuelta de Pecho
(chest turn)

Position = face front
Feet = 3rd, R front
Arms = 4th, L up

The footwork in the *Vuelta de pecho* is the same as for the *Vuelta normal*, but great care must be taken over the smooth transference of the weight and the equal distribution of weight from one foot to the other. If this is not strictly observed, balance can easily be lost when the body bends backwards.

PREPARATORY EXERCISES IN CO-ORDINATION

Before attempting the *Vuelta de pecho*, practise the previous exercise and really perfect the *Vuelta normal* so that the arms and feet are co-ordinated.

FEET

Count:

1   Moving to R, step into small 2nd with R
2   Cross L over R and stand with the weight equally distributed
a   Turn R on balls of feet with heels only just off the floor (begin to change weight on to L as the body faces the back),
3   finishing the turn facing front with weight on the L, R in *planta natural*

Take small steps, keeping the weight directly underneath the body as it makes the corkscrew bend. The turn should be smooth without rising up or down. Suggested practice is as follows:

1 *Vuelta normal*, 1 *Vuelta de pecho* to R and L.

Figs. 52, 53 & 54. *Vuelta de Pecho*. A.

ARMS

Count:

1 Looking front, change arms by passing through 2nd to 4th,

2 R up, at the same time bending to L (to front, as the body is now facing sideways with L shoulder towards the audience or mirror, continue to look front with R arm well behind head)

a Bend back with arms coming into 5th, top of head dropped back to audience, body facing upstage

3 R arm moves downwards into 1st as the turn finishes, with the arms in 4th, L up, the head having turned quickly to the R

You are now facing the front ready to make another turn.

ALTERNATIVE ARMS

1 5th

2 As the body bends forwards the arms move outwards from

Figs. 55, 56, 57 & 58. *Vuelta de Pecho.* B.

5th to 5th down behind, continuing the movement of arms through 5th front up to 5th as the body bends backwards
3   and turns to face front

Palmas y Pitos

Palmas, hand clapping, and *Pitos*, finger snaps, are used as an accompaniment to *flamenco* dances.

Palmas are used by the performer or by the accompanying artists

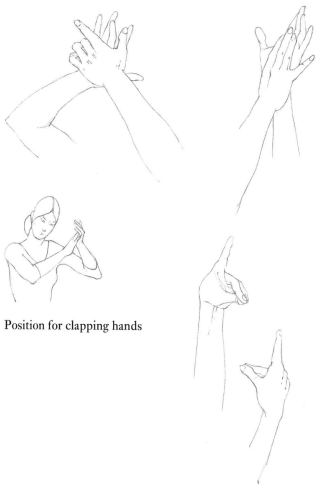

Position for clapping hands

Figs. 59, 60, 61 & 62. *Palmas and Pitos*

to inspire the dancer and to goad him or her to further invention or improvisation of rhythm and counter-rhythm.

The easiest clap to make is the quiet one. This is made by hollowing the palms of both hands and clapping them together in the same position as for *postiseo*, fingers curved and slightly apart. The sound will be muted. The loud clap is more difficult to make as it should be like a pistol shot. The easiest way to begin is to hollow the palm of the L hand using three fingers of the R, but separating the small finger.

Fit the three fingers into the hollow of the L palm, then strike the L palm sharply with the R three fingers, trying to fit neatly into the hollow. The hands should not be tense. The R hand should hit the L, the aim being to displace the air in the hollow with the sharpest possible sound. This requires a lot of practice. However, for the purpose of this manual the quiet clap is all you will need.

The position of the fingers for *Pitos* (finger snaps) is shown in Fig. 62. The sound should be sharp, alternating the L and R hands. The hitting of 2nd finger on to the 3rd finger and cushion of thumb produces the sound.

Basic flamenco rhythm

One *Compas* is counted as follows:
1 2 3, 1 2 3, 1 2, 1 2, 1 2.
Position = face front
Feet = 3rd, L front

FEET

Count:

1	Small step into 2nd with R
2	Beat ball of L in 4th front
3	Stand on L in 4th front
1	Continuing in
2	the same direction, keeping main weight on R,
3	repeat above
1	Small step into 2nd with R
2	Stand on L in 4th front
1	Small step into 2nd with R
2	Stand on L in 4th front

1   Small step into 2nd with R
2   Stand on L in 4th front

To make the quiet clap, hold the arms naturally in front of the chest without tension and without hiding the face.

Fig. 63. Basic *Flamenco* rhythm

− = rest

Palms	−	clap	clap	−	clap	clap	−	−	−	−	−	−
Count	1	2	3	1	2	3	1	2	1	2	1	2
Feet	R	L	L	R	L	L	R	L	R	L	R	L

You will have noticed that until now the clap has been made *on* the beat. Once this is perfected, the time has come to try clapping a counter-rhythm or *contra tiempo*. The first six counts are the same as before, followed by two foot beats without a clap. The contra-clap comes on the off-beat between the foot beats, finishing with a clap on the foot beat on the last beat of the bar. Execute as follows:

Palmas	–	clap	clap	–	clap	clap	–	–	clap
Count	I	2	3	I	2	3	I	2	a
Feet	R	L	L	R	L	L	R	L	

Palmas	–	clap	–	clap	–	clap
Count	I	a	2	a	I	2
Feet	R		L		R	L

Jerezana

Position = face front
Feet = in 3rd position, R in front
Arms = in 5th

FEET

Inclining the body to the R, point the R foot in the 4th front, then quickly lift R leg from below the knee backwards and sideways with a sharp upward kicking movement in order to raise the skirt.

Fig. 64. *Jerezana*

125

Count:

    &   In position

    a   point R, 4th front

    1   sharply lift R lower leg to kick up skirt

    2   hold

    3   step forward on R

    4   step forward on L

    5   step forward on R

    6   point L, 4th front, etc.

Repeat as above with L.

ARMS

Castanets	Count:	
	&	Arms in 5th
Postiseo	a	Arms in 5th
cop	1	R arm makes outwards circular
	2	movement to
	3	5th down
	4	continuing upwards movement to 5th
Postiseo	6	hold in 5th.
cop	1	Repeat as above with L.

LAS SEVILLANAS

Las Sevillanas is one of the best known regional dances both inside Spain and abroad. It is the Sevillian version of the *Seguidilla*.

The *Seguidilla* was born in La Mancha and its influence has spread throughout Spain, most of the regions having their own particular variation.

Although difficult to execute skilfully, the *Sevillanas* is one of the first dances to be taught to beginners in the dancing schools, possibly because the arm movements form one of the basic elements in classical Spanish dancing.

During the *Feria* in Seville, an annual Sevillian festival held six weeks after Easter, one has the best chance of seeing this dance performed in various ways, from good to indifferent. The following, slightly simplified, variation is the one generally used by professional dancers.

The *Sevillanas* consists of seven *coplas*, of which the first four are usually danced. They can be performed by a single couple or a number of couples of men and women or just girls.

The girl dances on the right side of the boy. A *copla* consists of the following:

Introduction and entrance, followed by three different figures which are joined by a passing step, finishing with a sustained pose.

The footwork, although lively, should be small, smooth and neat, with an occasional kick of the skirt.

The carriage of the upper part of the body, with the perpetually interweaving arms, plays an indispensable part in this dance. The continous arm movements, which should be both flowing and graceful, are the same as in the exercise *Braceo* I. They should be co-ordinated with those of the partner. It should be realised that the individual dancer only makes half the picture, therefore the beauty of the line is lost unless the arms of both dancers are synchronised.

The steps do not cover much ground. The dancers keep close together, bending their bodies towards and away, looking at each other while crossing and recrossing. The brilliant effect of this dance comes chiefly from the pattern made by the interchange of movement and position. In this simplified version the accent is always on count one, with the recurring forward *Sevillana* step coming on two. The timing is a guide for beginners.

Castanets for Las Sevillanas

It is sufficient to use the basic rhythm 'ta riá riá pi' (one bar) with a slight change on the *Entrada* which is indicated where necessary.

Begin by thoroughly learning the footwork of the *Entrada* and *Paseo Sevillana* before attempting the arms, as these steps recur throughout the dance.

Instead of counting, it may be found helpful to mark the rhythm by saying the castanet rhythm during early practice instead of actually playing. Having mastered the footwork, use the arms and lastly include the castanets.

LAS SEVILLANAS

Introduction = 8 bars of music (see Note on page 168)
Position   = relaxed, facing and looking at partner diagonally, R to R
Feet   = *Planta natural*, R in front
Arms   = L hand on L hip, R hitching skirt resting fingers on front of R thigh. Man holds front of jacket

Entrada (entrance) and 1st step of 1st Copla

FEET

Bars	Castanets	Count		
9	ta	1	Transfer weight on to R and kick back skirt with L	
	riá	2	Step forward 4th with L	
	pos.	3	Bring R to 3rd behind	
10	cop	1	Step back 4th behind with R	*Entrada*
	ta	2	Bring ball of L into 3rd front before	
	riápi	3	extending leg diagonally to L and	

LAS SEVILLANAS

11	ta	1	standing on L in 3rd behind	⎫
	riá	2	Forward 4th front with R	*Paseo*
	riápi	3	Bring L to 3rd behind	*Sevil-*
12	ta	1	Step back into 4th behind with L	*lana*
	riá	2	Bring ball of R into 3rd front before	⎭
	riápi	3	Extending leg to diagonal R	
13–18	ta etc.	1	Standing on R in 3rd behind	

Repeat *Paseo Sevillana* 4 times.

ARMS

Bars	*Count*	
9	1 2	Arms move forwards and upwards to
	3	5th
10	1 2	L arm makes outward circle to
	3	5th (note only 3 beats)
11	1 2	R arm makes outward circle as in *Braceo* 1
	3	to 5th down
12	1 2 3	R arm completes circle upwards to 5th.
13–18		The arms continue gracefully and smoothly in this way, alternately making an outward circular movement, until the end of *Paseo Sevillana* – always reaching the overhead position on the 6th beat.

FEET

Bars	*Count*	*Pasada* (passing step)
19	1	Step on L in 1st. These are marking steps
	2	Step on R in 1st
	3	Raise L leg in 4th front with knee flexed
20	1	2 steps forward to change places with partner LR
	2	R passing R shoulders
	3	Step on L making half turn to face partner (now on opposite side) finishing with the
9	1	weight on R in 3rd position front
	2	Repeat one *Sevillana* as before,
	3	5 beats in all . . .
10	1	
	2	
	3	Finish *Sevillana* with L leg extended to L.

129

ARMS

Bars	Count	
19	1	From 5th, both arms move inwards and
	2	downwards to 5th in front,
	3	continuing outwards and upwards to 5th as the body bends from the waist sideways to R, facing and looking at partner, R hip against R hip in momentary position before passing
20	1	R arm makes small outward circle
	2	as partners
	3	change places
9	1	
	2	
	3	As for *Paseo Sevillana*
10	1	
	2	
	3	

1st copla, 2nd step

FEET

Bars	Count	
11	1	Still facing partner, step on L in 3rd behind
	2	Travelling sideways to R, step on R in 2nd
	3	Step on L in 3rd front (i.e., ballet *pas de bourrée changé*) making quarter turn to R (partners should now face up/down stage)
12	1	Point R in 4th front
	2	Hold position
	3	Make small *developpé* (raise leg)
		Turning to face partner and travelling sideways to L
13	1	Step R
	2	Step L *Pas de bourrée changé*, as before
	3	Step R
14	1	Point L 4th front
	2	Hold position
	3	*Developpé* with L

130

15	1 2 3	Repeat 2nd step to R
16	1 2 3	
17	1 2 3	Repeat 2nd step to L
18	1 2 3	
19	1 2 3	*Pasada*
20	1 2 3	
21	1 2 3	*Sevillana*
22	1 2 3	
23	1 2	Lightly stamp L and R with feet together

1st copla, 2nd step

ARMS

Bars	Count	
11	1	The arms continue to move in the same way
	2	as in *Paseo Sevillana*, the R beginning the
	3	outward circle on *pas de bourrée changé*
12	1 2	reaching the 4th position as the foot points,
	3	and the 5th on *developpé*
13–23		On repeats arms continue to move as before

Note: On the last two beats of 2nd step the dancers are facing each other with their arms in 5th, then without moving their feet they make a quarter turn L away from each other, executing a *postiseo* before crossing to the opposite side to change places. They pass back to back with R arm up and L curved inwards by hip. The R arm moves smoothly to 5th down as the body turns R in place, ready to repeat this passing step. Forward, L arm up, passing L shoulders.

1st copla, 3rd step

FEET

Bars	Count	
	3*	With feet *en place* make quarter turn of the body to L (head, shoulders and arms)
24	1 2	Step forward on R, passing partner back to back and brushing L foot forward across R with flexed knee

* Note: The 3rd step starts on last beat of previous bar.

	3	Three small steps forward (changing places): L
25	I	R, L
	2	begin to make half turn to face partner
	3	Step R 4th behind (now facing partner)
26–31		Repeat this passing step three times (making four times in all), finishing the last step with weight on R, ready to make
32	I 2 3	*Vuelta normal* to L with L
		Make quarter turn to R, at the same time
33 chord	I 2 3	*golpe* R and point L 4th front (*planta natural*)
		Hold
		Stop suddenly and hold final position

1st copla, 3rd step

ARMS

Bars	Count	
(23)	3	*Postiseo* in 1st, looking at hand
24	I 2	In 3rd position, R up, L curved inward by hip, look R
	3	Arms in 4th down, R in front
25	I 2	Change to L in front
26–31		Crossing, turning *en place* and recrossing
		Repeat as above, omitting *postiseo*, finishing facing partner, arms in 4th, R up
32		As for *Vuelta normal*
33 (chord)		Pose, arms in 4th, looking at partner, L shoulder to L shoulder facing up and down stage

Note: The body leans backwards on the first two beats of the 3rd step, turning smoothly to face partner as the arms curve round the body, avoiding any angular movements.

2nd copla, introduction and 1st step
Musical introduction as before (8 bars).

FEET

Introduction: Dancers casually take up the same position as introduction to 1st *copla* (8 bars).

Bars	Count		
9–10			*Entrada* – Execute the first two bars as in 1st *copla*
11	1 2		Slightly stamp L and R feet together
		3	Pause
1ST STEP			
12	1		*Coupé** on L at the same time make
	2		a very small *rond de jambe á terre en dehors* to 2nd with R as body momentarily makes a quarter turn to R. Turn back to face partner, weight on R in
		3	3rd front.
13	1		Small marking step back to 3rd behind with L
	2		Small marking step back to 3rd behind with R
	3		Small marking step forward into 3rd in front with L
14–17			Repeat 1st step of 2nd copla to L and R
18	1 2 3		*Vuelta* normal to L wih L
19–	1 2 3		Repeat *Pasada* step as in 1st *copla*, fol-
20	1 2 3		lowed by
9	1 2 3		1 *Sevillana* etc. as before with a pause
10	1 2 3		on the last beat.
11	1 2 3		

*Step L and make small outward circle on the ground with R, ending in 3rd front.

ARMS

Bars	Count	
9–10		*Entrada* as in 1st *copla*
11	1 2	In 5th
	3	Pause

1ST STEP

Bars	Count	
12	1 2	R arm makes outward circle as the body makes quarter turn to R
	3	Face partner again
13	1 2 3	In 5th
14–17		Repeat 1st step L and R

Note : The arms move as in *Paseo Sevillana* with the R arm beginning its outward circle as the body turns R so that the dancers momentarily face up and down stage (L shoulder to L shoulder) with their arms in 4th on the *rond de jambe* before turning back to face each other as R arm reaches 5th. Hold this position on the small marked steps.

Bars	Count	
18	1 2 3	*Vuelta normal*
19–20		*Pasada . . .*
9–11		. . . finishing facing partner, arms in 5th

2nd copla, 2nd step

FEET

Bars	Count	
12	1	*Golpe* L (strong, with feet together)
	2 3	point R in 4th front (*planta natural*)
13	1	*golpe* R (strong, with feet together)
	2 3	point L, 4th front
14–17		Repeat with alternate feet 6 times in all
18	1 2 3	*Vuelta normal* to L with L
19–20		followed by Pasada and 1 Sevillana
21–23		etc. as in step 1 of this *copla*

ARMS

Bars	
12–17	As in *Paseo Sevillana*, but the movement is smaller and quicker as there are only 3 counts instead of 6 to complete the circles (6 in all). The arms finish in 5th on *Planta natural* excepting the 6th time, when they end in 4th (R up) ready to make the *Vuelta normal* followed by the pasada and 1
19–20	
21–23	*Sevillana* as in step 1 of this *copla*.

2nd copla, 3rd step

FEET

Bars	Count	
24	1 2 3	Move towards partner with R mark 2
25	1 2 3	very small *pas de basque* steps forward with feet together. On reaching partner (R hip to R hip) turn close together clockwise in place, with shoulders turned to face partner and head looking over R shoulder, which leads the turning.
26	1 2 3	*R*, L, R,
27	1 2 3	*L*, R, L, pivoting in place
28	1 2 3	*R*, L, R, with feet together
29	1 2 3	*L*, R, L,
		After making 1 or 2 pivots according to speed, each dancer turns outwards away from each other in a diagonal line to the R, making a
30	1 2 3	*vuelta de paso* with R to opposite diagonal corners
31	1 2 3	Maintaining the pose with weight on R, L shoulder facing L shoulder, with the L foot pointed naturally in the same diagonal line to partner. Body

135

facing sideways, chin over L shoulder in line with L foot, which is pointed towards partner, look L at partner:

32	1 2 3	Walk towards partner L, R, L,
33 (chord)	1 2 3	*Golpe* R, point L in 4th front. Hold.

ARMS

Bars	Count	
24	1 2 3	From 5th bring both arms inwards and
25	1 2 3	downwards to 5th in front,
26	1 2 3	bring gradually upwards through 2nd. continue upwards to 5th
27–29		In this position turn hip to hip gracefully to R in place with enough speed to make the skirt billow.
30	1 2 3	Arms in 4th down, R front
31	1 2 3	Changing smoothly to L front in pose, taking care to hold the body erect.
32	1 2 3	On walk to partner both arms come forwards through 1st (be careful not to drop arms on change of movement), to 4th with L behind head and R across chest. *Golpe* in diagonal line, looking at partner with the curved R arms almost touching on the final
33 chord	1 2 3	chord of music

3rd copla, introduction and 1st step

FEET

Bars	Count	
8 bars of Intro.		Introduction. (Optional, during which the partners turn outwards away from each other, walking in a small circle to return to their original places ready for the *Entrada*.)
9–10		*Entrada*, as in 2nd *copla*
11	3	*Golpe* with L in 3rd front

12	1 2 3	*Vuelta normal* with L, turning to L
13	1 2	Step on L to make a quarter turn, still to L (partners now face sideways, R shoulder to R shoulder)
	3	Beat ball of R in 3rd front ⎫ = 2 *Sostenidos*
14	1 2	Point R in 2nd to partner ⎪ *Note*: The first beat
	3	Beat ball of R in 3rd front ⎬ of the *Sostenidos* is
15	1 2	Point R in 2nd to partner ⎪ on the last beat of
	3	*Golpe* R in 3rd front ⎭ the previous bar
16–19		Repeat above to R from *vuelta normal* (4 bars)
20	1 2 3	Take 3 small steps forward L, R, L, passing partner, L shoulders, to change places
9–11		1 *Sevillana* etc.

ARMS

Bars	Count	
		Introduction: During optional walk round, the L hand is relaxed on hip (thumb at back) while the R arm swings forward naturally in opposition to the L foot
9–10		*Entrada*, as in 2nd *copla*
11	3	Arms in 5th
12	1 2 3	Quickly open both arms outward
13	1 2 3	through 2nd to 5th down, then up
14		through 1st, 2nd, 4th with L up. Dur-
15		ing *Sostenidos* incline from the waist sideways towards partner, looking over R shoulder
16–19		Repeat to R, with R up in 4th, inclining towards partner and looking over L shoulder
20	1 2 3	R arm down
9–11		As for *Sevillana*

3rd copla, 2nd step

FEET

Bars	Count	
(11)	3	Making a quarter turn to R, step on L in 3rd behind to walk forward
12	1 2 3	R, L and bring feet together (partners face up and down stage to move in opposite directions)
13	1 & a 2	*Redoble* with R
	3	Step on R in 3rd behind, turning and travelling to L, walk
14	1 2 3	L, R and bring feet together
15	1 & a 2	*Redoble* with L
	3	Repeat to R, stepping on L in 3rd behind
16	1 2 3	
17	1 2 3	
18	1 2 3	*Vuelta normal* with L, turning to L
19–20		*Pasada*
21–23		1 *Sevillana*, etc.

ARMS

Bars	Count	
(11)	3	
12–	& a 1 2 3	On walk to side the arms are in 4th down, beginning with the R in front, gradually
13	1 & a 2 3	changing to L in front, on the *redoble*, holding this position and looking at partner.
14–	& a 1 2 3	Repeat with L in front to L as above
15	1 & a 2 3 a	Repeat with R in front as above
16–17		As an alternative, the girl's skirt can be held while moving the arms as described above, taking care to hold up the elbows. The man can hold his jacket, also keeping the elbows up.

18	1 2 3	The arms are as for *vuelta* step
19–20		*Pasada*
21–23		1 *Sevillana* etc.

3rd copla, 3rd step

FEET

Bars	Count	
(23)	3	*Postiseo*, as in 3rd step of 1st *copla*
24	1 2 3	Repeat 3rd step of 1st *copla* once (when partners pass back to back). Partners should have changed places, having made 1 complete turn *en place*, standing L hip to L hip with weight on L, facing up and down stage and
25	1 2	leaning slightly away from each other
	3	Beat ball of R in 3rd behind
26	1 2	Make *Sostenidos* with R to 4th behind
	3	5th behind
27	1 2	Repeat *Sostenidos*
	3	*Postiseo* and
28–31		Repeat all to L
32	1 2 3	Change weight on to L, still keeping weight directly under the body
33 Chord	1 2 3	Change weight on to R, hold position

ARMS

Bars	Count	
(23)	3	*Postiseo* to side as in 3rd step of 1st *copla*
24–	1 2 3	Repeat 3rd step of 1st *copla* once
25	1 2	
	3	In 4th down, L arm in front, holding this
26	1 2 3	position for *Sostenidos*, looking at partner
27	1 2	with elbows up and relaxed arms
	3	*Postiseo*
28–31		Repeat all to L

32	1 2 3	Drop arms loosely at side, subtly shaking the shoulders (R shoulder to R shoulder)
33 Chord	1 2 3	Pose, L arm overhead, R round partner's waist, the L arm moved quickly upwards through 2nd to 5th as R held waist

4th copla, introduction and 1st step

FEET

Bars	Count	
8 bars of music		Introduction: As for 3rd *copla*
9–11		*Entrada*: As for 3rd *copla*
(11)	3	*Golpe* L, 3rd front (on last beat of bar)
12	1 2 3	*Vuelta normal*, turning to L with L
13	1	weight on L in 4th front
	2 3	1 *Sevillana*
14	1 2 3	to R with R
15	1 2	*Pas de bourrée changé en place* with R (i.e., very small step in 3rd behind, step 1st with L)
	3	*Golpe* R, 3rd front
16	1 2 3	*Vuelta normal*, turning to R with R
17	1	weight on R in 4th front
	2 3	1 *Sevillana* to L
18	1 2 3	
19–20		*Pasada*
9–11		1 *Sevillana* etc.

ARMS

Bars	Count	
8 bars		Introduction: As for 3rd *copla*
9–11		*Entrada*: As for 3rd *copla*
(11)	3	5th, *Postiseo*
12	1 2 3	Arms open outwardly through 2nd to 1st

13—	I			In 1st
	2	3		As *Sevillana*
14	I	2	3	As *Sevillana*
15	I	2		Open both arms outwardly, from 5th to 1st
			3	In 1st
16	I	2	3	Hold 1st for *vuelta*, ending with R up for
17—	I	2	3	1 *Sevillana*
18	I	2	3	
19—20				*Pasada*
9—11				1 *Sevillana*

4th copla, 2nd step

FEET

Bars	*Count*	
		Preparing to change places,
12	I	dancers take a large step forward with L, at the same time turning quarter R to face each other and bending sideways to R (the backs of the dancers face up and down stage)
	2	Slide R through 1st to 4th behind
	3	Put weight on L, beginning to turn L
13	I	Step on R with back to partner
	2	Step on L, finishing turn to L
	3	Step on R, now facing partner

The movement is like a long waltzing step to change places, followed by a small waltzing step turning *en place*.*

14	I	2	3	*Pas de basque en place* to L
15	I	2	3	*Pas de basque en place* to R
16	I	2	3	Repeat *careo* (face to face step)
17	I	2	3	
18	I	2	3	*Vuelta normal*, turning to L
19—20				*Pasada*
21—23				1 *Sevillana* etc.

*This step is called *careo*, meaning fact to face.

ARMS

Bars	Count	
		Arms in 5th, preparing for *careo* (face to face step)
		The arm movement is similar to that in *Paseo Sevillana*
12	1 2 3	– a big well-marked circle should be made with the R arm on the large waltzing step look R followed by a
13	1 2 3	smaller, less marked one with the L, look at partner
14	1 2 3	R arm makes outward circle to 5th, look L
15	1 2 3	L arm makes outward circle to 5th, look R
16	1 2 3	As for *careo*
17	1 2 3	
18	1 2 3	As for *vuelta*
19–20		*Pasada*
21–23		1 *Sevillana*

4th copla, 3rd step

FEET

Bars	Count	
24–31		Increasing speed, make 4 continuous well-marked *careos*, followed by
32	1 2 3	*vuelta normal* turning to L, plus quarter turn to L, ready for final
Chord 33	1 2 3	*golpe* R, point L 4th front

ARMS

Bars	Count	
24–31		As for *Careo*
32	1 2 3	As for *Vuelta normal*, turning to L
33 Chord	1 2 3	Arms in 4th, outside arms up, both facing audience.
		Partners hold final pose looking at each other, or one can kneel if preferred.

THE FANDANGO

The *Fandango*, of which there are many variations, is supposed to have its origin in popular Moorish songs. The version from Huelva is based on an Andalusian folk tune in 3/8 time, usually performed by a group of men and girls playing castanets, accompanied by singers and guitarists. It can also be danced as a solo.

The following version for girls, although arranged for the piano, is *flamenco* in style. Graceful, flowing movements alternate with *taconeo* and some *contra tiempo*.

The timing is typically Spanish, which in the beginning you may find a little difficult. Often the first step begins on the last beat of the previous bar, as in the introductory step, so take special note of the beats where they are indicated. The basic movement is *Braceo* I, both outwards and inwards. Sometimes the change of position is made by one arm moving inwards while the other moves upwards and outwards. The arms should be relaxed and supple, without tension, especially during contrasting strong movements of the feet. The wrists and fingers should be flexible and the whole arm movement controlled to weave slowly and smoothly round the body.

FANDANGO DE HUELVA

Piano intro: 17 bars
Play castanet intro: in position
Position   = face partner diagonally, R shoulder to R shoulder
Feet   = 3rd position, R in front
Hands   = hold naturally in front of body, playing castanets

Castanet introduction

Bars	Count					Bars	Count			
18	{ I,	a 2,	a 3,	a,		24	{ 1, a	2, a	3,	
	{ ta,	riá,	riá	pi			{ á,	riá,	pita	
19	{ I,	a 2,	a 3,			25	{ I,	2,	a 3,	a
	{ ta,	riá,	riá	pi			{ —	ta,	riá,	ri . . .
20	{ I,	a 2,	a 3			26	{ I,	a 2,	a 3,	
	{ ta,	riá,	riá,				{ á,	Riá,	pita	
21	{ I,	2,	a 3,	a		27	{ I,	2,	a 3,	a
	{ —	ta,	riá,	ri . . .			{ —	ta,	riá,	ri . . .
22	{ I,	a 2,	a 3,			28	{ I,	a 2,	a 3,	
	{ á,	riá,	pita				{ a,	riá,	riá,	
23	{ I,	2,	a 3,	a						
	{ —	ta,	riá,	ri . . .						

Introductory step to 1st copla

FEET

Bars	Count	
29	1 & a 2 3	*Redoble*, starting with L
30	1	Hold
	2	Beat ball of R foot in 3rd front
	3	Beat ball of R foot in 2nd
31	1	Hold
	2	Beat ball of R foot in 3rd front
	3	Beat ball of R foot in 2nd
32	1	Hold
	2	Small step with R to R almost in place
	3	Hold
33	1	Small step with L to R
	2	Small step in place with R
		(Repeat all with L to L, starting . . .)
	3	Beat ball of L foot in 3rd front, etc.

34–37

This introductory step consists of two well-marked strong *Sostenidos* followed by three small smooth walks taking you, still facing partner, to the opposite diagonal position, i.e., L shoulder to L shoulder. You may find the timing a little difficult, so note the 'rest' and accentuated beats.

ARMS

Bars	Count	
29	1 2	5th behind
30	3 1	Raise arms to 4th, L up
	2	Hold
	3	Hold
31	1	Hold
	2	Hold
	3	Hold
32	1	Hold
	2	Gradually bring L arm inwards through
	3	1st while R moves outwards and
33	1	upwards into 4th position, R up
	2	
	3	Arms are now in 4th position, R up. Be sure to show the correct position with upheld elbows and curved arms, which should move smoothly together
34–37		Repeat with L to L

Summary of introductory step to 1st copla

Bars	Count	Castanets	Feet	Arms
29	1 &	—	Redoble	5th down behind
	a 2	—	—	
	3	—	—	Raise arms to 4th L up
30	1	—	—	
	2	ta	Beat R in 3rd front	
	3	riá	Beat R in 2nd	
31	1	—	—	
	2	ta	Beat R in 3rd front	
	3	riá	Beat R in 2nd	
32	1	—	—	
	2	ta	Small step to R with R	Gradually
	3	riá	Hold	change

Bars	Count	Castanets	Feet	Arms
33	1	ta	Small step to R with L	to 4th,
	2	riá	Step in place with R	R up
	3	—	Beat L in 3rd front	
33–37	Repeat *Sostenidos* with L to L			

1st copla, 1st step

Position = face partner
Feet = 1st

FEET

Bars	Count	
38	1 ⎫	R forward to 4th front, inclining weight on
	2 ⎬	ball of slightly turned out foot
	3 ⎭	Hold
39	1 ⎫	R foot returns to closed 1st position
	2 ⎬	Hold
	3 ⎭	Hold
40		Repeat
41		with L
42–49		Then alternately (6 times in all)

The feet move smoothly forwards and together with a sinuous, relaxed style of hip movement. The body is upright, leaning slightly backwards as the foot moves forward – head held high, looking at partner.

ARMS

The arm movement is the same as in *Braceo* I.

Bars	Count	
		In 5th
38	1 2 3	Make outward circular movement with R arm
39		
	1 2 3	Complete the continuous circular movement upwards to 5th
40		Repeat
41		with L
42–49		Then alternately

The arms should pass through the positions in a continuous graceful movement, reaching the half circle down and the completed circle on the count 3.

Clearly show the 5th position with both arms together overhead before the L arm begins its outward circle.

1st copla, 1st step – summary

Bars	Count	Castanets	Feet	Arms
38	1	Cop	R forward into 4th	R makes
	2	ta	Hold	outward circle
	3	riá	Hold	to 5th down
39	1	Cop	R moves back to 1st	R completes
	2	ta	Hold	upward circular
	3	riá	Hold	movement to 5th
40–49		Repeat 6 times in all		

1st copla, 2nd step

Position	= face partner
Feet	= 1st
Arms	= 5th
Look	= At partner and away from working arm as you step back

FEET

Bars	Count	
Last beat		
of 49	3	1 golpe with L
50	1 2	Step on L, raising R knee*
	3	Stand on R in 4th front
51	1	Step back with L into 4th behind
	2	Bring R back into 1st with
	3	1 golpe R, to
52–57		Repeat whole step 4 times in all

*The object of sharply raising the knee upwards towards the chin is to make the skirt fly up, showing the flounces. The toe should be by the knee of supporting leg. The body must not move up and down with the working leg, but should appear still except for natural, sinuous hip movements.

147

ARMS

The arms move smoothly inwards and outwards, circling round the body in a continuous movement. On the repeat the L arm moves inwards as R moves outwards and upwards to opposite position.

Bars	Count	
Last beat of 49	3	In 5th
50	1	Moves L inwards and downwards in a curved position through 1st until fingers are poised over L hip
	2 3	Hold
51	1 2	Move R inwards and downwards curved through
	3	1st until R hand is poised over R hip
52–57	1 2 3	L moves outwards and upwards to 5th on repeat, then as above. Repeat 4 times

1st copla, 2nd step – summary

Bars	Count	Castanets	Feet	Arms
Last beat of 49	3	—	*Golpe* L	5th
50	1	—	Stand on L	L down
	2	ta	Raise R knee	to
	3	riá	Stand on R	L hip
	a	pi	—	R down
51	1	ta	Step back on L	to
	2	—	—	R
	3	—	*Golpe* R	hip
52	1	—	Stand R	L up
	2	ta	Raise L knee	R to
	3	riá	Stand on L	R hip
	a	pi	—	L down
53	1	ta	Step back on R	to
	2	—	—	L
	3	—	*Golpe* L	hip
54–57		Repeat of step		

Simple vuelta quebrada

1st copla, 2nd step (continued)

Position = facing partner
Feet   = In 1st
Arms   = both hands poised over hips

FEET

Bars	Count	
Bars	*Count*	
58	1	Step on L in 1st (in place)
	2 3	Slide R forward into 4th front
59	1	Change weight on to L, make small circle
	2	outwardly on the ground with R (*rond de jambe a terre en dehors*)
	3	Cross R behind L (toes forward, weight equal, as in *Vuelta normal*)
60	1 2 3	Turn R, finish with weight on L, bring R to 1st
61	1 2 3	Pause

ARMS

Bars	Count	
Bars	*Count*	
		Hands poised over hips
58	1	Both arms move gracefully
	2 3	outwards through 2nd into 4th, L up
59	1	Change to opposite position, both arms
	2 3	moving outwards through 2nd to 4th, R up
60	1	Moving simultaneously, keeping the arms
	2	curved, the R moves inwards and downwards
	3	through 1st and L moves upwards to 4th
61	1 2 3	Raise R arm to 5th

Simple vuelta quebrada – summary

1st copla, 2nd step (continued)

Bars	Count	Castanets	Feet	Arms
58	1	ta	Step on L	Through 2nd
	2	riá	Slide R to	change to
	3	riá	4th front	4th, L up

THE FANDANGO

Bars	Count	Castanets	Feet	Arms
59	1	riá	Circle	through 2nd
	2	riá	outwardly R	to
	3	riá	Cross R behind L	4th, R up
60	1	riá	Turn	Move to
	2	riá	to	L up
	3	riá	R	R down
61	1	—	⎫	Raise R
	2	—	⎬ Pause	to
	3	—	⎭	5th

Pasada

1st copla, 3rd step

Facing partner, arms 5th

FEET

Bars	Count	
62	1	Step with R to diagonal 4th behind
	a 2	Bring ball of L to 3rd front
	a 3	Slightly raise L foot to diagonal 4th front
63	a 1	Stand on L in 3rd behind
	a 2	Step forward with R and
	a 3	bring L into 3rd behind (this should bring you in line with partner, L shoulder to L shoulder)
64	a 1	Step on L in place as you make a half turn to R (you have now changed places and should face partner on opposite side)
	a 2	Bring ball of R to 3rd front
	a 3	Raise R in 4th front (on repeat bring feet together)
65	1	Stand on R in 3rd behind
	2	Step forward with L
	3	Bring R into 3rd behind
66–68		Repeat 1st 3 bars of the above *pasada* step
69	1 & a 2	*Redoble* L, R, R, L
	3	Hold
		Now repeat introductory step to 1st *copla*, from *Sostenidos* on beat 2 of the 2nd bar.
70–77		

ARMS

Bars	Count				
					5th
62	I	2	3		L arm makes outward circle back to 5th
63	I	2	3		R arm makes outward circle to 5th down
64	I	2	3		R arm completes circle upwards to 5th
65	I	2	3		L arm makes outward circle to 5th down
66	I	2	3		L arm completes circle upwards to 5th
67	I	2	3		R arm makes outward circle to 5th down
68	I	2	3		R arm completes circle upwards to 5th
69	I	&	a	2	Arms down to 5th behind
	3				Raise arms to 4th, L up, ready for repeat of introductory step to 1st copla
70–77					

Pasada

1st copla, 3rd step – summary

Bars	Count	Castanets	Feet	Arms
62	a	—	—	L makes
	I	ta	Step back on R	outward
	a	ri ⎫		
	2	á ⎬	L foot to 3rd front	circle
	a	ri ⎫		back
	3	á ⎬	Slightly lift L	to 5th
	a	pi		R makes
63	I	ta	Stand on L	outward
	a	ri ⎫		half
	2	á ⎬	Forward R	circle
	a	ri ⎫		to
	3	á ⎬	L to 3rd behind	5th down
	a	pi		R
64	I	ta	Step on L ½ turn R	completes
	a	ri ⎫		
	2	á ⎬	R to 3rd front	circle
	a	ri ⎫		to
	3	á ⎬	Lift R	5th
	a	pi		L makes

Bars	Count	Castanets	Feet	Arms
65	I	ta	Stand on R	outward
	a	ri		half
	2	á }	Forward with L	circle
	a	ri		to
	3	á }	R to 3rd behind	5th down
66–68			Repeat 1st 3 bars as above	
	a	—		Both arms
69	I	—	*Redoble* L	5th
	&		R	down
	a		R	behind
	2	—	L	
	3	—	Pause	4th, L up

70–77   The introductory step to the 1st *copla* is now repeated, starting from the *Sostenidos*.

2nd copla, 1st step

12 bars   Execute 3 *escobillas* as in the exercise, except that you begin by facing your partner instead of the audience, travelling up and down stage instead of in a diagonal line. Having travelled to the L on the first 2 bars, partners should turn and face each other and be fairly close together on the 2nd beat of the 3rd bar. Avoid taking large steps. In other words, the dancers work and look towards each other, though moving in opposite directions.

Work and look away, then turn to face each other (up and downstage) with feet together.

The *pas de bourré* takes them back to their original position, ready to repeat the *escobilla* to the R.

ESCOBILLA (BRUSHING STEP)
Position = face partner
Feet = 3rd, L front
Arms = in 5th
Dancing up and down stage.

FEET

Bars	Count	
78	1 2 3	Step on L, brush and point R through 1st into 4th front
79	1 2	Step on R in 4th
	3	progressing forwards, brush L in 4th front and point
80	1	Take a very small step sideways on L and face partner
	2	Bring feet together
	3	Step upstage with R
81	1	Step L 3rd front ⎫ Small *Pas de*
	2	Step R very small 2nd ⎬ *Bourré changé*
	3	Step L 3rd behind ⎭ almost in place
82–89		Repeat all to R and again to L, 8 bars

ARMS

Bars	Count	
78	1 2 3	4th position, L overhead, in diagonal line to L corner
79	1 2 3	Change inwards to R overhead, through 1st
80	1 2	Bring to 5th
	3	Hold
81	1 2 3	L arm moves inwards. The position is now 4th with R overhead
82	1 2 3	Hold
83–89		Repeat to R and L

The arms should move smoothly and gracefully from one position to the next. In the diagonal 4th, remember to hold the arm well behind the head, with the front arm curved across the chest, so that a straight diagonal line is made with the pointing foot.

Look at partner on the first bar of *escobilla* (3 beats), then towards the direction in which you are travelling on the second bar; look back at partner on the third and fourth bars of music, dropping the eyes on the *pas de bourré*, during which the small movement should make the skirt swirl in a figure of eight.

Practise feet, arms and castanets separately, then feet and arms together, then feet and castanets together.

Lastly, when you have mastered all separately, try all three together.

2nd copla, 1st step – summary

Bars	Count	Castanets	Feet	Arms
78	1	ta	Travelling up and down stage, step L	In 4th, L overhead.
	2	ta	Travelling up and down stage, brush R	Hold
	3	riá	Travelling up and down stage, point R	Hold
79	1	ta	Travelling up and down stage, step R	Change inwards
	2	ta	Travelling up and down stage, brush L	to 4th
	3	riá	Travelling up and down stage, point L	R overhead.
80	1	ta	step on L	In 5th.
	2	postiseo	bring feet together facing partner	In 5th
	3	cop	step back on R	In 5th
81	1	ta	step on L, 3rd front	L moves
	2	riá	step on R, small 2nd	inwards to
	3	riá pi	step on L, 3rd behind back to position	4th, R up (hold for next 3 beats)

82–89 Repeat to R and L

2nd copla, 2nd step

Partners make quarter turn to R (L shoulder to L shoulder), looking at each other but working in a straight line away from each other towards the side of the stage, making the following
(This step is the same as the first two bars of the exercise Basic *Flamenco* Rhythm):

FEET

Bars	Count	
90	1	Step 2nd with R
	2	Beat L on ball of foot in 4th front
	3	Stand on L

91	1 2 3	Repeat
92	1	*Golpe* R
	2 3	*2 golpes* L
93	1	Pause
	a 2	*Golpe* R, L
	3	*Golpe* R
94–95		Repeat 1st two bars
96	1 2	Put weight on R and bring feet together, facing partner. The following steps are executed travelling forwards with very small shuffling steps on the flat foot, catching the heel on the floor at the end of each step.
	a	Shuffle L
	3	Shuffle R
	a	Shuffle L
97	1	Shuffle R
	a	Shuffle L
	2 3	Feet together
97–100		Execute as before the step called Simple *Vuelta Quebrada*
101		Pause

ARMS AND HEAD

Bars	*Count*	
90	1 2 3	Bring R arm into the 4th down position, L in front
91	1 2 3	Hold, at the same time slowly circling both wrists outwardly and inwardly
92	1 2 3	Change through 2nd to 4th down, R in front (look quickly to R). Hold position
93	1 2 3	Change to 4th down, L in front (look at partner)
94–95		Repeat
96	1 2	Swing arms back to 5th behind
	a 3	Relaxed, feeling
97	a 1	the tips of the fingers as the arms move forwards
	a 2 3	through 1st upwards to 5th
98–100		For the repeat of the Simple *Vuelta Quebrada* the arms are as described
101	1 2 3	Raise to 5th

2nd copla, 2nd step – summary

Bars	Count	Castanets	Feet	Arms
90	1	—	Step 2nd R	4th down, L in front
	2	—	Beat L in 4th	Hold position
	3	—	Stand on L	looking at partner
91	1	—	Slowly step 2nd R	Circling wrists
	2	—	Beat L in 4th	
	3	—	Stand on L	
92	1	—	*Golpe* R	
	2	—	*Golpe* L	Change to 4th down, R in front
	3	—	*Golpe* L	Look R
93	1	—	Pause	Hold
	a	—	*Golpe* R	Hold
	2	—	*Golpe* L	Hold
	3	—	*Golpe* R	Change to 4th down, L in front
94–95		Repeat 1st 2 bars of the above		
96	1	—	Feet together	Swing back to 5th behind
	2	—	—	—
	a	—	Slide L	Gradually move forward
	3	—	Slide R	to 5th
	a	—	Slide L	in front
97	1	—	Slide R	Through 1st upwards
	a	—	Slide L	to 5th then to
	2	—	Feet together	4th, L up, for the
	3	—	Hold	repeat of
98–100				Simple *Vuelta Quebrada*
101			Pause	Raise to 5th

2nd copla, 3rd step

Bars	
102–108	Repeat *Pasada* (3rd step of 1st *copla*) followed
109–117	by a repeat of the Introductory step

3rd copla, 1st step

Having repeated the *Pasada* and Introductory step, partners make a quarter turn to R (L shoulder to L shoulder), progressing forwards anticlockwise with small steps in a tight circle, keeping close to partner. Then facing outwards and inwards on 'flick' of skirt, make the following step called *jerezana*:

FEET

Bars	Count	
(117)	1 2	
	3	Point R in 4th front, in this position
118	1	turn R knee inwards, at the same time
	2	lift R foot outwards and upwards to flick the
	a	skirt towards the outside of circle
	3	Small step forward R
119	1	Small step forward L
	2	Small step forward R
	3	Point L 4th front, in this position turn L knee
120	1	inwards, at the same time lift L foot upwards
	2	to flick skirt towards partner
	3	Step forward L
121	1	R
	2	L
122–129	3	Repeat the *jerezana* 6 times. This will bring you back to your original position after having made 2 circles, then turn to face audience ready for the next step.

Note: Be careful to mark well the last and first beats.

ARMS

Bars	Count	
		The dancers stand shoulder to shoulder, facing up and downstage, with arms in 5th. As they progress, the outside arms move smoothly downwards while the inside arms remain above the dancers' heads. Avoid jerking the arms on the 'flick'.

Bars	Count		
117	1 2	5th	
	3	*Postiseo* in 5th (look forwards)	
118	1 2	R arm makes outward circle to (look R)	
	3	5th down in front	
119	1 2	R completes circle to 5th (look forwards)	
	3	*Postiseo* in 5th (look forwards)	
120	1 2	L arm makes outward circle to (look L)	
	3	5th down in front	
121	1 2	L completes circle to 5th (look forwards)	
	3	*Postiseo* in 5th	
122–129		Repeat *jerezana* 6 times	

3rd copla, 1st step – summary

Bars	Count	Castanets	Feet	Arms
(117)	3	*Postiseo*	Point R	5th
118	1	cop	Flick R	Circle outwardly with R
	2	ta	Hold	to
	3	riá	Step R	5th down
	a	pi		
119	1	ta	Step L	Complete upward
	2	riá	Step R	circle
	3	*postiseo*	& point L	to 5th
120	1	cop	Flick L	Circle outwardly
	2	ta	Hold	with L
	3	riá	Step L	to
	a	pi		5th down
121	1	ta	Step R	Complete upward
	2	riá	Step L	circle to 5th
	3	*postiseo*	Repeat *jerezana* to R and L	
122–129			6 times in all	

3rd copla, 2nd step

Positions = face audience, standing side by side
Arms = 5th

THE FANDANGO

FEET

Bars	Count		
130	1	Stepping on L ⎤	With feet together, mark
	2	Beat ball of R ⎟	rhythm by gently moving
	3	Hold ⎟	the hips from side to side
131	1	Step on R ⎟	with a natural swinging
	2	Beat ball of L ⎟	motion. Avoid exaggerated
	3	Hold ⎦	movements, keeping the
			upper part of the body still
132–137		Repeat the above step (8 bars in all) strongly marking the rhythm and moving slightly forwards	

ARMS

Bars	
130–137	Arms move inwards from 5th to 5th down in front, then slowly outwards and upwards through 2nd to reach the 5th position during eight bars of music. Avoid bringing the arms too close to the body on the inward movement, which must be kept flowing.

3rd copla, 2nd step – summary

Bars	Count	Castanets	Feet	Arms
130	1	ta	Step on L	From 5th
	a	ti		move
	2	ta	Beat R	inwards
	a	ti		to 5th
	3	ta	Hold	down
	a	ti		
131	1	ta	Beat R	Raise slowly
	a	ti		outwards
	2	ta	Beat L	and upwards
	a	ti		reaching
	3	ta	Hold	the 5th position
	a	ti		after 8 bars
				of music
132–137	The above step is repeated (8 bars in all)			

3rd copla, last step

FEET

Bars	Count	
		Turn to face partner and prepare for *Vuelta quebrada* by
138	1 2 3	putting weight on L and sliding R into 4th front
139	1 2 3	Make a small outward circle with R (*rond de jambe a terre*) to R crossed behind L weight equally divided
140	1 2 3	Turn R, finishing with R in 3rd front
141	1 2 3	1 *Vuelta normal* to R in place, finishing
142	1	quarter turn R to face audience
	2	Hold
	3	Step forward with inside foot, keeping weight equally divided between the feet
143	1	Hold
	2	Step forward with outside foot
	3	Hold
144	*1* 2 3	Point inside foot 4th front (*planta natural*), leaving weight on back foot.

The last movement consists of two deliberate steps forward, followed by a pose. It is essential for the feet, arms and head to be co-ordinated exactly on the accented beats *3, 2, 1*.

ARMS

Bars	Count	
138	1 2 3	Small outward circle with R, finishing 4th, L up
139	1 2 3	Both arms move through 2nd into 4th, R up
140	1 2 3	Change through 1st to 4th, L up
141	1 2 3	Lower to 4th down, L front, changing to
142	1	R front at end of turn (face audience shoulder to shoulder)
	2	
	3	Partners' outside arms move outward and upwards through 2nd to 5th. Inside arms remain curved by hip (look forward)

143	1		
	2		Inside arms move upwards through 2nd to 5th (look forward)
	3		Both arms move downwards to 4th down, inside arm forward
144	1 2 3		Look at partner

Note: By small outward circle it is meant that the working arm is taken to shoulder level.

3rd copla, last step – summary

Bars	Count	Castanets	Feet	Arms
138	1	ta	Step on L	Small outward circle
	2	riá	Slide R	with R
	3	rià pi	to 4th front	to 4th, L up
139	1	ta	Small outward	Both arms move
	2	riá	circle with R	through 2nd to
	3	riá pi	Cross R behind L	4th, R up
140	1	ta	Turn to R	Change through
	2	riá	finishing	1st to
	3	riá	Front R in 3rd	4th, L up
141	1	ta	Vuelta to R	Lower to 4th down, L front
	2	riá	Turn to R	change to
	3	riá pi	turn finishes	R front
142	1	ta	Turn to face front	R front
	2	—	Pause	
	3	cop	Step forward (inside foot)	Outside arms overhead
143	1	—	Hold	Inside arms move upwards
	2	cop	Outside forward	to 5th
	3	—	Hold	Both arms down to 4th in front
144	1	cop	Step forward with inside foot	4th down, inside arm in front
	2	—	Pose	in front
	3	—	Pose	Hold

GLOSSARY

Alegría	*Flamenco* dance (*Cante Jondo*)
À terre (Fr)	on the ground
Baile	dance
Baile de Escuela	school dance
Baile de Zapatilla	slipper dance
Baile chico	gay or frivolous 'little dance'
Baja	down
Balloné (Fr)	lift leg and bend knee with hop
Battement (Fr)	see *Destaque*
Bolero	18th-century slipper dance
Bolero liso	alone, solo
Bolero de medio paso	half pace
Bolera con Cuchacha	with *Cuchacha*
Bolero popular	popular
Bolero robado	stolen
Braceo	carriage of the arms
Bulería	*flamenco* dance (allied to *Cante Chico*)
Café Cantante	see *Tablao*
Cambios	jumps with changes of feet
Campanela	raise thigh (diagonal front), circling lower leg
Caña	*Flamenco* dance (allied to *Cante Chico*)
Cante Chico	light songs of the Spanish gipsies
Cante Jondo	profound songs of the Spanish gipsies
Caracoles	*Flamenco* dance (allied to *Cante Chico*)
Careo	pass partner, facing each other

Caretilla	roll on the castanets
Changement de pied (Fr)	change of feet
Clásico	classical
Clásico Español	Spanish classical dancing
Compas	bar of music
Contra Tiempo	counter rhythm
Cop	beat on both castanets played together
Copla	verse
Cortados	cutting step
Cuadro Bolero	group of *Bolero* dancers
Cuadro Flamenco	group of *Flamenco* dancers
Cuatro	four
Cuña	rocking step
Delante	in front
Demi plié (Fr)	half bend knees, keeping heels on ground
Demi pointe (Fr)	half toe stand on ball of foot, with extended instep
Desplante	rhythmic phrase to close section of *flamenco* music
Destaque	like *grande battement*, slide leg upwards from closed position
Detras	behind
Developpé (Fr)	slow unfolding of the working leg until fully extended
Doble	double
Dos	two
Ecarté (Fr)	diagonal 2nd
Echado	*jeté* or throwing step
Emboteados	cut front foot to back, as *retiré*
En dedans (Fr)	inwards
En dehors (Fr)	outwards
En l'air (Fr)	in the air
En place (Fr)	in place
Entrada	entrance
Escobilla	brushing step
Escuela Bolero	18th-century slipper dances
Fandango	type of Spanish dance

Farruca	*Flamenco* dance, usually for a man (*Cante Chico*)
Féria	fair or festival
Flamenco	Andalusian gipsy music, song and dance
Fin	end
Garrotin	*Flamenco* dance (Valls gipsies)
Golpe	beat
Golpeando	sharp beats on castanets
Granadillo	pomegranate wood (used for castanets)
Hembra	female
Huelva	Andalusian town associated with *Fandango*
Jaleo	Classical dance
Jerezana	point foot and flick skirt upwards
Jota	type of dance (the best known is from Aragon)
Lazos	alternating changing of feet by rotating leg with bent knees
Lizadas	*glissade* (Fr), sliding step
Macho	male
Malagueña	step; also regional dance from Malaga
Ocho	eight
Olé	classical dance
Palillero	castanet carver
Palmas	hand claps
Pasada	passing step
Pas de bourré changé (Fr)	commonly used in Spanish classical and regional dance (for the purposes of this manual, step L behind, step R to 2nd bring L 5th in front)
Paseo	series of steps, as in *paseo Sevillana*, etc.
Paso	step
Paso de Vasco	*pas de Basque*, commonly used in Spanish classical and regional dances

Pasodoble	popular Spanish two-step
Peteneras	step and name of *flamenco* dance
Petits Tours (Fr)	series of turns
Pita	single beat on R then L castanet
Pitos	finger snaps
Planta natural	standing on back foot, with the front foot in 4th position resting on ball
Pointe tendu (Fr)	pointed foot with extended instep
Postiseo	strike castanets together
Punta y tacon or talon	toe and heel
Rasgueando	continuous fluid roll
Redoble	four heel beats
Relever (Fr)	to rise on the half toe
Retiré (Fr)	see *Emboteados*
Riá	roll with R castanet, finishing with single beat on L
Rodozan, Ronds de jambe (Fr)	circle in the air with lower leg
Rumbitas	*Flamenco* dance of Cuban origin
Seguidilla	name and type of dance
Seguiriyas	serious *Flamenco* song and dance (allied to *Cante Jondo*)
Sencilla	simple
Sevillanas	regional dance from Seville, name of step
Siete	seven
Soleares	*Flamenco* dance (allied to *Cante Jondo*)
Sostenido	sustained pointing step
Ta	Single beat with L castanet
Tablao	*Flamenco* cabaret
Tacon	heel of shoe
Taconeo	heel beats
Talon	heel of foot
Tangos	*Flamenco* dance (allied to *Cante Chico*)
Ti or Pi	single beat on R castanet
Tiempos	time, beats
Tipico	typical

Tres	three
Vuelta	turn
Vuelta normal	ordinary turn
Vuelta de paso	stepping turn
Vuelta de pecho	chest turn
Vuelta quebrada	(simple) like *vuelta normal* in reverse
Zambra	*Flamenco* dance of Moorish origin
Zapateado	rhythmic beats with both heels and ball of foot
Zapato	derived from the Arabic, meaning shoe
Zapatilla	flat shoe used in classical Spanish dances
Zarzuela	light Spanish opera, name of a theatre in Madrid

BIBLIOGRAPHY

ARMSTRONG, LUCILE, *Dances of Spain, I and II*, Chanticleer Press, 1939, New York.

BONALD, CABALLERO, *Andalusian Dances*, Editorial Noguer, Barcelona, 1959.

BORRUL, TRINI, *La Danza Espanola*, Sucesor E Mesuquer, Barcelona.

CLARAMUNT, ALFONSO PUIG, *Ballet y Baile Español*, Montaner y Simon, S.A., Barcelona, 1944.

IVANOVA, ANA, *El Alma Español y el Baile*, Editoria National, Madrid.

MATTEO, *Woods that Dance*, Dance Perspectives 33, Spring 1965, New York, 29 East 9th St. New York.

LA MERI, *Spanish Dancing*, Eagle Printing & Binding Co., Pittsfield, Mass. 1967.

POHREN, DONN E, *The Art of Flamenco*, Editorial Jerez Industrial, Jerez de la Frontera, 1962.

TRIANA, FERNANDO EL DE, *Arte y Artistas Flamencos*, Clan Madrid, 1935.

MUSIC

Music for the exercises and dances can be obtained from:

United Music Publishers, 42 Rivington Street London EC2. Some of the music mentioned in this manual is in a book called *Coleccion de Bailes Españoles* by Garcia Navas including the *Sevillanas Populares*. The version of the latter used as our example is called *Fuentes* (*Trianeras*) on page 5. This has an eight bar introduction which ends with a double bar line repeat sign. The following *entrada* and *Copla* consist of 12 bars of the same music repeated three times with a single chord to finish each *copla*. A different air, from pages 6, 7 or 2, should be chosen for each *copla* of Sevillanas.

The *Fandango de Huelva* is traditional music arranged for the piano by *Modesto Romero* and is sold separately as are several pieces of music mentioned in the text. The publishers are Union Musical Española, San Geronimo 26, Madrid, Spain.

The *coplas* of both dances can be adapted for guitar accompaniment.